WEST-E® Social Studies Skill Practice

Practice Test Questions for WEST-E® Social Studies Test

Published by

Complete TEST Preparation Inc.

Copyright © 2015 by Complete Test Preparation Inc. ALL RIGHTS RESERVED.

No part of this book may be reproduced or transferred in any form or by any means, graphic, electronic, or mechanical, including photocopying, recording, web distribution, taping, or by any information storage retrieval system, without the written permission of the author.

Notice: Complete Test Preparation Inc. makes every reasonable effort to obtain from reliable sources accurate, complete, and timely information about the tests covered in this book. Nevertheless, changes can be made in the tests or the administration of the tests at any time and Complete Test Preparation Inc. makes no representation or warranty, either expressed or implied as to the accuracy, timeliness, or completeness of the information contained in this book. Complete Test Preparation Inc. make no representations or warranties of any kind, express or implied, about the completeness, accuracy, reliability, suitability or availability with respect to the information contained in this document for any purpose. Any reliance you place on such information is therefore strictly at your own risk.

The author(s) shall not be liable for any loss incurred as a consequence of the use and application, directly or indirectly, of any information presented in this work. Sold with the understanding, the author is not engaged in rendering professional services or advice. If advice or expert assistance is required, the services of a competent professional should be sought.

The company, product and service names used in this publication are for identification purposes only. All trademarks and registered trademarks are the property of their respective owners. Complete Test Preparation Inc. is not affiliated with any educational institution.

We strongly recommend that students check with exam providers for up-to-date information regarding test content.

WEST-E,® and Washington Educator Skills Test are registered trademarks of the Wahington Professional Educator Standards and Board and Pearson Education, who are not involved in the production of, and do not endorse this publication.

Published by
Complete Test Preparation Inc.
921 Foul Bay Rd.
Victoria BC Canada V8S 4H9
Visit us on the web at http://www.test-preparation.ca
Printed in the USA

ISBN-13: 978-1772450323 (Complete Test Preparation Inc.)
ISBN-10: 1772450324

Version 6.5 February 2015

About Complete Test Preparation

The Complete Test Preparation Team has been publishing high quality study materials since 2005. Thousands of students visit our websites every year, and thousands of students, teachers and parents all over the world have purchased our teaching materials, curriculum, study guides and practice tests.

Complete Test Preparation is committed to providing students with the best study materials and practice tests available on the market. Members of our team combine years of teaching experience, with experienced writers and editors, all with advanced degrees.

Feedback

We welcome your feedback. Email us at feedback@test-preparation.ca with your comments and suggestions. We carefully review all suggestions and often incorporate reader suggestions into upcoming versions. As a Print on Demand Publisher, we update our products frequently.

Find us on Facebook

www.facebook.com/CompleteTestPreparation

The Environment and Sustainability

Environmental consciousness is important for the continued growth of our company. In addition to eco-balancing each title, as a print on demand publisher, we only print units as orders come in, which greatly reduces excess printing and waste. This revolutionary printing technology also eliminates carbon emissions from trucks hauling boxes of books everywhere to warehouses. We also maintain a commitment to recycling any waste materials that may result from the printing process. We continue to review our manufacturing practices on an ongoing basis to ensure we are doing our part to protect and improve the environment.

Contents

- **6** **Getting Started**
  - The WEST-E® Social Studies Study Plan — 7
  - Study Tips for Computer Based Tests — 12
- **13** **Practice Test Questions Set 1**
  - Answer Key — 48
- **83** **Practice Test Questions Set 2**
  - Answer Key — 118
- **152** **Conclusion**

Getting Started

CONGRATULATIONS! By deciding to take the WEST-E® Social Studies Test, you have taken the first step toward a great future! Of course, there is no point in taking this important examination unless you intend to do your very best in order to earn the highest grade you possibly can. That means getting yourself organized and discovering the best approaches, methods and strategies to master the material. Yes, that will require real effort and dedication on your part but if you are willing to focus your energy and devote the study time necessary, before you know it you will be on you will be passing your exam with a great mark!

We know that taking on a new endeavour can be a little scary, and it is easy to feel unsure of where to begin. That's where we come in. This study guide is designed to help you improve your test-taking skills, show you a few tricks of the trade and increase both your competency and confidence.

About the Exam

The WEST-E® Social Studies test is composed of four main sections, US and world history, geography, civics and government and economics. The exam is computer based. See below for tips on taking a computer based exam.

While we seek to make our guide as comprehensive as possible, it is important to note that like all exams, the WEST-E Social Studies test might be adjusted at some future point. New material might be added, or content that is no longer relevant or applicable might be removed. It is always a good idea to give the materials you receive when you register to take the WEST-E® Social Studies a careful review.

The WEST-E® Social Studies Study Plan

Now that you have made the decision to take the WEST-E® Social Studies, it is time to get started. Before you do another thing, you will need to figure out a plan of attack. The very best study tip is to start early! The longer the time period you devote to regular study practice, the more likely you will be to retain the material and be able to access it quickly. If you thought that 1x20 is the same as 2x10, guess what? It really is not, when it comes to study time. Reviewing material for just an hour per day over the course of 20 days is far better than studying for two hours a day for only 10 days. The more often you revisit a particular piece of information, the better you will know it. Not only will your grasp and understanding be better, but your ability to reach into your brain and quickly and efficiently pull out the tidbit you need, will be greatly enhanced as well.

The great Chinese scholar and philosopher Confucius believed that true knowledge could be defined as knowing both what you know and what you do not know. The first step in preparing for the WEST-E® Social Studies is to assess your strengths and weaknesses.

Making a Study Schedule

To make your study time most productive you will need to develop a study plan. The purpose of the plan is to organize all the bits of pieces of information in such a way that you will not feel overwhelmed. Rome was not built in a day, and learning everything you will need to know to pass the WEST-E® Social Studies is going to take time, too. Arranging the material you need to learn into manageable chunks is the best way to go. Each study session should make you feel as though you have succeeded in accomplishing your goal, and your goal is simply to learn what you planned to learn during that particular session. Try to organize the content in such a way that each study session builds on previous ones. That way, you will retain the information, be better able to access it, and review the previous bits and pieces at the same time.

Self-assessment

The Best Study Tip! The very best study tip is to start early! The longer you study regularly, the more you will retain and 'learn' the material. Studying for 1 hour per day for 20 days is far better than studying for 2 hours for 10 days.

What don't you know?

The first step is to assess your strengths and weaknesses. You may already have an idea of where your weaknesses are, or you can take our Self-assessment modules for each of the areas, Reading Comprehension, Arithmetic, Essay Writing, Algebra and College Level Math.

Exam Component	Rate 1 to 5
History	
US History	
World History	
Geography	
Civics and Government	
Economics	

Making a Study Schedule

The key to making a study plan is to divide the material you need to learn into manageable size and learn it, while at the same time reviewing the material that you already know.

Using the table above, any scores of three or below, you need to spend time learning, going over and practicing this subject area. A score of four means you need to review the material, but you don't have to spend time re-learning. A score of five and you are OK with just an occasional review before the exam.

A score of zero or one means you really do need to work on this and you should allocate the most time and give it the highest priority. Some students prefer a 5-day plan and others a 10-day plan. It also depends on how much time you have until the exam.

Here is an example of a 5-day plan based on an example from the table above:

US History: 1   Study 1 hour everyday – review on last day
World History: 3   Study 1 hour for 2 days then ½ hour and then review
Geography: 4   Review every second day
Economics: 2 Study 1 hour on the first day – then ½ hour everyday
Civics and Government: 5   Review for ½ hour every other day

Using this example, economics and Civics and Government are good, and only need occasional review. Geography is good and needs 'some' review. World History needs a bit of work and US History is very weak and need most of the time. Based on this, here is a sample study plan:

Day	Subject	Time
Monday		
Study	US History	1 hour
Study	Economics	1 hour
	½ **hour break**	
Study	World History	1 hour
Review	Geography	½ hour
Tuesday		
Study	US History	1 hour
Study	Economics	½ hour
	½ **hour break**	
Study	World History	½ hour
Review	Geography	½ hour
Wednesday		
Study	US History	1 hour
Study	Economics	½ hour
	½ **hour break**	
Study	World History	½ hour
Thursday		
Study	US History	½ hour
Study	Economics	½ hour
Review	World History	½ hour
	½ **hour break**	
Review	Geography	½ hour
Friday		
Review	US History	½ hour
Review	Economics	½ hour
Review	World History	½ hour
	½ **hour break**	
Review	Geography	½ hour
Review	Economics	½ hour

Using this example, adapt the study plan to your own schedule. This schedule assumes 2 ½ - 3 hours available to study everyday for a 5 day period.

First, write out what you need to study and how much. Next figure out how many days you have before the test. Note, do NOT study on the last day before the test. On the last day before the test, you won't learn anything and will probably only confuse yourself.

Make a table with the days before the test and the number of hours you have available to study each day. We suggest working with 1 hour and ½ hour time slots.

Start filling in the blanks, with the subjects you need to study the most getting the most time and the most regular time slots (i.e. everyday) and the subjects that you know getting the least time (e.g. ½ hour every other day, or every 3rd day).

Tips for making a schedule

Once you make a schedule, stick with it! Make your study sessions reasonable. If you make a study schedule and don't stick with it, you set yourself up for failure. Instead, schedule study sessions that are a bit shorter and set yourself up for success! Make sure your study sessions are do-able. Studying is hard work but after you pass, you can party and take a break!

Schedule breaks. Breaks are just as important as study time. Work out a rotation of studying and breaks that works for you.

Build up study time. If you find it hard to sit still and study for 1 hour straight through, build up to it. Start with 20 minutes, and then take a break. Once you get used to 20-minute study sessions, increase the time to 30 minutes. Gradually work you way up to 1 hour.

40 minutes to 1 hour is optimal. Studying for longer than this is tiring and not productive. Studying for shorter isn't long enough to be productive.

Study Tips for Computer Based Tests

The WEST-E Social Studies test is a Computer based, exam, which is just like the pencil-and-paper exam but digital.

The first tip, which applies to either type of exam, is to use your scratch paper. Computer based tests do not allow you to jump around. The test questions are displayed in a set sequence. Use your scratch paper to make notes, copy diagrams, or anything else you feel will help you answer the questions that follow.

Other Tips and Strategies

There are several tips and strategies that can help you perform well on both the computer-based and computer-adaptive exams.

Practice. Practicing the test gives you the chance to see the types of questions that are asked, as well as providing you an opportunity to see how the test looks.

Complete the test tutorials. Most exams have a computer tutorial for test-takers immediately before the exam. Make sure you take the time to go through it. The tutorial is not timed, and it will walk you through the process of taking the computer-based exam. Even though you probably know how to use a computer and it may seem unnecessary, do the tutorial. Make sure you know everything you possibly can about what you are about to do!

Be aware of the time. The test is timed. Typically, there is an on-screen clock that counts down the remaining time and alerts you when you are down to five minutes. Pace yourself so you can finish each section in the allotted time.

Practice Test Questions Set 1

The questions below are not the same as you will find on the WEST-E® Social Studies test - that would be too easy! And nobody knows what the questions will be and they change all the time. Below are general questions that cover the same subject areas as the WEST-E® Social Studies test. So, while the format and exact wording of the questions may differ slightly, and change from year to year, if you can answer the questions below, you will have no problem with the WEST-E® Social Studies test.

For the best results, take these practice test questions as if it were the real exam. Set aside time when you will not be disturbed, and a location that is quiet and free of distractions. Read the instructions carefully, read each question carefully, and answer to the best of your ability.
Use the bubble answer sheets provided. When you have completed the practice questions, check your answer against the Answer Key and read the explanation provided.

Do not attempt more than one set of practice test questions in one day. After completing the first practice test, wait two or three days before attempting the second set of questions.

World History Answer Sheet

1. (A) (B) (C) (D)   11. (A) (B) (C) (D)
2. (A) (B) (C) (D)   12. (A) (B) (C) (D)
3. (A) (B) (C) (D)   13. (A) (B) (C) (D)
4. (A) (B) (C) (D)   14. (A) (B) (C) (D)
5. (A) (B) (C) (D)   15. (A) (B) (C) (D)
6. (A) (B) (C) (D)   16. (A) (B) (C) (D)
7. (A) (B) (C) (D)   17. (A) (B) (C) (D)
8. (A) (B) (C) (D)   18. (A) (B) (C) (D)
9. (A) (B) (C) (D)   19. (A) (B) (C) (D)
10. (A) (B) (C) (D)   20. (A) (B) (C) (D)

US History Answer Sheet

1. Ⓐ Ⓑ Ⓒ Ⓓ   11. Ⓐ Ⓑ Ⓒ Ⓓ
2. Ⓐ Ⓑ Ⓒ Ⓓ   12. Ⓐ Ⓑ Ⓒ Ⓓ
3. Ⓐ Ⓑ Ⓒ Ⓓ   13. Ⓐ Ⓑ Ⓒ Ⓓ
4. Ⓐ Ⓑ Ⓒ Ⓓ   14. Ⓐ Ⓑ Ⓒ Ⓓ
5. Ⓐ Ⓑ Ⓒ Ⓓ   15. Ⓐ Ⓑ Ⓒ Ⓓ
6. Ⓐ Ⓑ Ⓒ Ⓓ   16. Ⓐ Ⓑ Ⓒ Ⓓ
7. Ⓐ Ⓑ Ⓒ Ⓓ   17. Ⓐ Ⓑ Ⓒ Ⓓ
8. Ⓐ Ⓑ Ⓒ Ⓓ   18. Ⓐ Ⓑ Ⓒ Ⓓ
9. Ⓐ Ⓑ Ⓒ Ⓓ   19. Ⓐ Ⓑ Ⓒ Ⓓ
10. Ⓐ Ⓑ Ⓒ Ⓓ   20. Ⓐ Ⓑ Ⓒ Ⓓ

Geography Answer Sheet

1. A B C D
2. A B C D
3. A B C D
4. A B C D
5. A B C D
6. A B C D
7. A B C D
8. A B C D
9. A B C D
10. A B C D
11. A B C D
12. A B C D
13. A B C D
14. A B C D
15. A B C D
16. A B C D
17. A B C D
18. A B C D
19. A B C D
20. A B C D

Civics and Government Answer Sheet

1. A B C D   11. A B C D
2. A B C D   12. A B C D
3. A B C D   13. A B C D
4. A B C D   14. A B C D
5. A B C D   15. A B C D
6. A B C D   16. A B C D
7. A B C D   17. A B C D
8. A B C D   18. A B C D
9. A B C D   19. A B C D
10. A B C D   20. A B C D

Economics Answer Sheet

1. Ⓐ Ⓑ Ⓒ Ⓓ   11. Ⓐ Ⓑ Ⓒ Ⓓ
2. Ⓐ Ⓑ Ⓒ Ⓓ   12. Ⓐ Ⓑ Ⓒ Ⓓ
3. Ⓐ Ⓑ Ⓒ Ⓓ   13. Ⓐ Ⓑ Ⓒ Ⓓ
4. Ⓐ Ⓑ Ⓒ Ⓓ   14. Ⓐ Ⓑ Ⓒ Ⓓ
5. Ⓐ Ⓑ Ⓒ Ⓓ   15. Ⓐ Ⓑ Ⓒ Ⓓ
6. Ⓐ Ⓑ Ⓒ Ⓓ
7. Ⓐ Ⓑ Ⓒ Ⓓ
8. Ⓐ Ⓑ Ⓒ Ⓓ
9. Ⓐ Ⓑ Ⓒ Ⓓ
10. Ⓐ Ⓑ Ⓒ Ⓓ

Social Studies Skills and Concepts

1. A B C D   11. A B C D
2. A B C D   12. A B C D
3. A B C D   13. A B C D
4. A B C D   14. A B C D
5. A B C D   15. A B C D
6. A B C D   16. A B C D
7. A B C D   17. A B C D
8. A B C D   18. A B C D
9. A B C D   19. A B C D
10. A B C D   20. A B C D

Part I - World History

1. What is an early human civilization that smelted copper and alloyed it with tin?

    a. The Tin Age

    b. The Bronze Age

    c. The Stone Age

    d. The Iron Age

2. Which of these are NOT a trait of Classical Greece (4th and 5th centuries BCE)?

    a. The Punic Wars

    b. The Persian Wars

    c. The Parthenon

    d. The philosopher Socrates

3. What political practice, that still influences governments today, was started in Classical Greece?

    a. Dictatorship

    b. Communism

    c. Capitalism

    d. Democracy

4. What are Ares, Aphrodite, Demeter and Athena examples of?

    a. Greek gods

    b. Roman gods

    c. Egyptian gods

    d. Norse gods

5. Which of these did NOT contribute to the fall of the Roman Empire?

   a. The spread of Christianity

   b. Political instability

   c. Invasion by Egyptian forces

   d. Over reliance on slave labor

6. What is/are the Vedas in ancient Indian history?

   a. A time period in which the region saw great economic, social and religious freedom.

   b. The ruling class

   c. A group of people who took over the original Harappan people of India.

   d. Texts discussing the history and religion of Indian peoples and transmitted orally.

7. What was the first recorded Chinese dynasty?

   a. Xia Dynasty

   b. Han Dynasty

   c. Tang Dynasty

   d. Qing Dynasty

8. Which of these inventions were NOT invented by the Chinese?

   a. Paper making

   b. Chemical warfare

   c. Gunpowder

   d. Calculus

9. Which religion allows people to follow the Eightfold Path to Nirvana?

    a. Buddhism
    b. Hinduism
    c. Islam
    d. Taoism

10. What major religion emerged through the prophet Muhammad in Arabia in 7th century CE?

    a. Christianity
    b. Islam
    c. Judaism
    d. Zoroastrianism

11. Which of these factors was NOT important in the development of European Nation States?

    a. Breaking of the Catholic Church from the state in England
    b. Establishment of national languages
    c. Napoleon Bonaparte in France
    d. Centralization of European governments

12. Which of the following was the main reason for mass migrations into Western Europe during the Dark Ages?

    a. Violence in Eastern Europe that caused people to flee
    b. Rapid increases in population that forced people to migrate
    c. Economic and agricultural prosperity in Rome that encouraged others to move there
    d. Refusal of Roman elite to support the military that would have stopped migration

13. Which invention was a cause of the Renaissance in Europe?

    a. The steam engine which allowed mass transportation of goods

    b. The flying shuttle which increased cloth production

    c. The printing press which increased production of books

    d. Concave and convex lenses which led to the development of eye glasses, microscopes, and telescopes

14. Which important Renaissance figure wrote Utopia?

    a. Thomas More

    b. Niccolo Machiavelli

    c. Martin Luther

    d. Nicholas Copernicus

15. Which of these was NOT a result of the Renaissance in Europe?

    a. Increased appreciation for reason, the arts and sciences.

    b. Weakening of the authority of the Church.

    c. Weakening of the authority of the monarchy.

    d. Increased the use of local languages.

16. What did an increased spirit of inquiry by the people, interference by the Pope in non-religious matters and selling of indulgences by the Church led to?

    a. The Renaissance

    b. The Reformation

    c. The Scientific Revolution

    d. The Protestant Revolution

17. Which of these was NOT a result of the Reformation?

    a. The creation of the Protestant sect of the Christian Church

    b. The Thirty Years' War

    c. Increased power of the monarchy

    d. An end to religious prosecution

18. What is Martin Luther most famous for?

    a. Breaking free of the Church and supporting the formation of Presbyterian churches

    b. Preaching for religious tolerance during the Reformation

    c. Writing the 95 theses in 1517 that attacked the Church

    d. Writing Utopia in 1516

19. Which key figure of the Scientific Revolution was responsible for the discovery of the laws of planetary motion that later influenced Isaac Newton?

    a. Johannes Kepler

    b. Galileo Galilei

    c. Francis Bacon

    d. Rene Descartes

20. Who introduced the heliocentric view of the universe?

    a. Nicholas Copernicus

    b. Tycho Brahe

    c. Francis Bacon

    d. Isaac Newton

Part II - US History

1. Which one of these was not part of the Intolerable Acts?

    a. The Stamp Act

    b. The Townshed Acts

    c. The Tea Act

    d. The Foreign Trade Act

2. The British American colonists revolted because

    a. most colonists wanted to be free from British rule.

    b. most colonists wanted to be represented in Parliament.

    c. most colonists did not want to be taxed.

    d. All of the Above

3. Why did the British Parliament impose the first of the Intolerable Acts?

    a. To raise revenue for British Parliamentary salaries

    b. To pay for the British military in the American Colonies

    c. To make trade with non-British countries more expensive

    d. To fund the British military's ongoing war in India

4. What was the last plea to Great Britain to avert the American Revolutionary War?

    a. The Olive Branch Petition

    b. The Dove Accords

    c. Jefferson's Plea

    d. Adam's Plea

5. Why did the First Continental Congress meet?

    a. Respond to the Intolerable Acts
    b. Establish a military
    c. Establish a federal government
    d. Address issues of states rights

6. Why did the Second Continental Congress meet?

    a. Establish a federal government
    b. Respond to the Intolerable Acts
    c. Ask for aid from the French
    d. Establish a military

7. What document announced a state of war between the British American colonists and Great Britain?

    a. The Articles of Confederation
    b. The Declaration of Independence
    c. The United States Constitution
    d. The Declaration of Hostilities

8. Which of these was NOT considered part of Manifest Destiny?

    a. American people and institutions are special
    b. America had a mission to turn the west into an agrarian landscape
    c. America's destiny was to settle the west
    d. All of the above are correct

9. What was the start of western expansion?

    a. The Clermont steamboat
    b. The Mexican American War
    c. The invention of the telegraph
    d. The discovery of gold in California

10. When did the Gold Rush start in California?

    a. 1849

    b. 1848

    c. 1855

    d. 1851

11. Which was the largest land acquisition for the United States?

    a. The Louisiana Purchase

    b. The Treaty of Guadalupe Hidalgo

    c. The Texas Annexation

    d. The Gadsden Purchase

12. Which State was once a nation with its own president before joining the Union during westward expansion?

    a. Delaware

    b. California

    c. Alaska

    d. Texas

13. What most shortened the time it took for people to travel across the United States during westward expansion?

    a. The telegraph

    b. The Clearmont steamboat

    c. The Transcontinental Railroad

    d. The Northwest Passage

14. What marked the end of western expansion?

a. Arizona statehood

b. The end of the Mexican American War

c. The Completion Speech

d. The President William Mckinley's Assassination

15. What was the Trail of Tears?

a. The last bloody battle/retreat of the Sioux Nation westward

b. The forced removal of Irish immigrants from New York

c. The relocation of many Native American tribes to "Indian Territory"

d. The portion of the Transcontinental Railroad that claimed the most lives during constuction

16. Who did Jacksonian Democrats believe should be able to vote?

a. White males

b. All males

c. Everyone

d. Landed gentry

17. The Second Great Awakening was

a. a multi-denominational religious movement to prepare people for the "End of Days."

b. a Reaction against religion, and the rise of logic over faith.

c. a religious movement against skepticism and rationalism

d. a movement aimed toward reducing corruption in politics and putting politicians in power to support the "everyman."

18. In what case did Chief Justice John Marshal most increase the powers of the Supreme Court?

    a. Fletcher v. Peck

    b. Marbury v. Madison

    c. Brown v. Board of Education

    d. Roe v. Wade

19. Which of these was NOT a purpose of the Lewis and Clark Expedition?

    a. Explore and map the Louisiana purchase

    b. Find a practical route to the Pacific Ocean

    c. Establish American presence in the Louisiana Territory

    d. Try to claim some of the adjoining Spanish territory

20. Which of these is true about the First Barbary War?

    a. The United States fought the war because they were the only country forced to pay a tribute to the Barbary States

    b. It was the first time the United States fought a war in a foreign land

    c. Spain suggested that the United States should fight or the Barbary Pirates would demand more tribute for safe passage

    d. The United States decisively beat the Barbary pirates and took back American prisoners without having to pay any tribute or ransom

Part III - Geography

1. Which of the following is not a reason humans move to urban areas?

    a. Excitement

    b. Education

    c. Open spaces

    d. Job opportunities

2. The era of human existence before writing was developed is known as

    a. Ancient history

    b. Prehistory

    c. Recorded history

    d. Unknown history

3. A thin stretch of land that connects two large areas of land is called

    a. a glacier.

    b. a peninsula.

    c. an isthmus.

    d. an ice sheet.

4. What is an ecosystem?

    a. a group of environmentalists that fight pollution

    b. a group of living organisms and their surrounding environment

    c. a law that delineates city zones

    d. a set of protocols that ensure environmental sustainability

5. Which ocean borders the east coast of Africa?

    a. Atlantic

    b. Indian

    c. Arctic

    d. Pacific

6. Cuba, Haiti and Puerto Rico are located in the

    a. Caribbean Sea.

    b. North Sea.

    c. Indian Ocean.

    d. Black Sea.

7. The Ural Mountains separate the continents of

    a. North and South America.

    b. Africa and Asia.

    c. Australia and Asia.

    d. Europe and Asia.

8. Australia is a very large

    a. continent.

    b. ocean.

    c. island.

    d. peninsula.

9. A nation is also known as

    a. a country.

    b. a government.

    c. a society.

    d. a utopia.

10. Which of the following is shown most clearly on a physical map?

    a. the borders of countries

    b. the movements of various populations

    c. the ruins of ancient civilizations

    d. features such as mountains, lakes and rivers

11. Which of the following is shown most clearly on a political map?

    a. The borders of countries

    b. The movements of various populations

    c. The ruins of ancient civilizations

    d. Features such as mountains, lakes and rivers

12. The study of human movements and the development of society is known as

    a. biology.

    b. archeology.

    c. anthropology.

    d. paleontology.

13. The study of artifacts from the past is known as

    a. biology.

    b. archaeology.

    c. anthropology.

    d. paleontology.

14. The connection of different societies through technology such as the telephone, cellular phone and internet is known as

    a. the first agricultural revolution.

    b. the industrial revolution.

    c. the second agricultural revolution.

    d. the communications revolution.

15. Globalization refers to the

    a. education of all people around the world.

    b. connection of all of the economies of the world.

    c. large colonial empires of England and Spain.

    d. the study of ancient civilizations.

16. Which of the following is a brief definition of Geography?

    a. The study of lands, features and phenomena of the Earth

    b. The study of the phenomena of the Earth

    c. The study of the physical features of the Earth

    d. None of the above

17. What are Area studies?

    a. The study of physical features in a specified area

    b. The study of human-land relationships

    c. The study of natural phenomena in a specified area

    d. None of the above

18. What are two branches of Geography?

   a. Human geography and physical geography
   b. Planet geography and social geography
   c. Earth Science and area studies
   d. None of the above.

19. What is environmental geography?

   a. Interactions between the environment and humans
   b. A combination of physical and human geography
   c. Study of the environment
   d. None of the above

20. What is Geomorphology?

   a. The study of landforms
   b. The study of physical features of the earth.
   c. The study of topographical and bathymetric features of the Earth
   d. None of the above.

Part IV Civics and Government

1. What is a political system with a king or queen as leader?

   a. Monarchy
   b. Republic
   c. Democracy
   d. Utopia

2. The concept of voting dates back to

    a. The Enlightenment.

    b. The American Revolution.

    c. Ancient civilizations.

    d. The Renaissance.

3. How is government conducted under a dictatorship?

    a. A strong leader is held responsible to the will of the people

    b. Elected representatives from different parties compromise to create laws

    c. Authority rests with the people

    d. A strong ruler is not held responsible to the will of the people

4. What concept gives a government supreme power within its own territory?

    a. Nationalism

    b. Sovereignty

    c. Justice

    d. Liberty

5. What is a government controlled by the wealthy?

    a. A democracy

    b. A dictatorship

    c. A monarchy

    d. An plutocracy

6. The ancient Romans had a legislative branch of government known as the

    a. Emperor
    b. President
    c. Supreme Court
    d. Senate

7. What is a government controlled by elected representatives?

    a. A Republic
    b. Utopia
    c. A Monarchy
    d. A Oligarchy

8. The primary purpose of the Magna Carta was to

    a. Limit the power of the English peasants.
    b. Limit the power of the English Parliament.
    c. Limit the power of the English Military.
    d. Limit the power of the English King.

9. What is a government controlled by religious leaders based on adherence to a religion?

    a. plutocracy
    b. monarchy
    c. anarchy
    d. theocracy

10. What is a constitution?

    a. a document that outlines the principles and structure of a government
    b. a document that summons citizens to court
    c. a document that petitions the government for grievances
    d. a document that abolished slavery

11. What is a confederation?

   a. a strong central government

   b. a loosely-tied group of states

   c. a dictatorship

   d. a theocracy

12. Which of the following is not listed in the Preamble to the U.S. Constitution as a purpose for government?

   a. To form a more perfect union

   b. To claim land that belongs to the United States

   c. To provide for the common defense

   d. To establish justice

13. Karl Marx wrote that most struggles in the world are struggles between

   a. the people and their governments.

   b. religious institutions and their governments.

   c. children and their parents.

   d. rich people and poor people.

14. The majority of governments currently are

   a. monarchies.

   b. democracies.

   c. autocracies.

   d. dictatorships.

15. Which of the following states was not part of the original thirteen colonies?

   a. Nebraska

   b. Virginia

   c. Georgia

   d. New York

16. At the time of the American Revolution, the English government was a

a. constitutional monarchy.

b. theocracy.

c. dictatorship.

d. democracy.

17. Which of the following were not a cause of the American Revolution?

a. New political philosophies becoming popular in the American Colonies

b. The institution of slavery

c. Harsh taxes by the English government

d. The Boston Massacre

18. For hundreds of years, England has had a legislative branch of government known as

a. Parliament.

b. Congress.

c. The Senate.

d. The Supreme Court.

19. What universal rights are listed in the Declaration of Independence?

a. life, education, health

b. literacy, happiness, freedom

c. health, wealth, the pursuit of happiness

d. life, liberty, the pursuit of happiness

20. The first ten amendments to the U.S. Constitution are also known as the

    a. Bill of Rights

    b. Declaration of the Rights of Man

    c. Human Rights Act

    d. Declaration of Independence

Part V - Economics

1. As demand increases, supply tends to

    a. decrease.

    b. increase.

    c. remain the same.

    d. fluctuate.

2. As supply increases, prices tend to

    a. rise.

    b. fall.

    c. remain the same.

    d. fluctuate.

3. As economy of scale increase, products are

    a. expensive to produce at first, but eventually become less expensive.

    b. cheap to produce at first, but eventually become more expensive.

    c. expensive to produce because they are customized to individual customers.

    d. sold to the highest bidder.

4. Which of the following is true of a free market economy?

a. The government owns the resources but allows citizens to own private property.

b. The government owns the resources and does not allow citizens to own private property.

c. Resources and private property are owned by citizens.

d. Resources are owned by citizens, but not private property.

5. Which of the following is true of a command economy?

a. The government owns the resources but allows citizens to own private property.

b. The government owns the resources and does not allow citizens to own private property.

c. Resources and private property are both owned by citizens.

d. Resources are owned by citizens, but not private property.

6. What is capital?

a. A measure of individual income.
b. The head of a company, also known as the CEO.
c. The resources needed to start or expand a business.
d. A meeting place for a company's board of directors.

7. What is inflation?

a. An expansion of business
b. An increase in the value of money
c. A decrease in the value of money
d. A growth in unemployment

8. A country's labor force excludes

    a. employees that work as professionals

    b. employees that are not union members

    c. employees that are union members

    d. children that are too young to work

9. Which of the following is a good example of a blue collar occupation?

    a. Miner

    b. Professor

    c. Scientist

    d. Accountant

10. What is consumer confidence?

    a. The optimism held by the general public regarding the economy.

    b. The trust that consumers have that the products they buy are safe.

    c. The demand for a product.

    d. The marketing used to make products seem valuable.

11. Unemployment figures do not include

    a. white collar labor markets

    b. former government employees

    c. people who lost their jobs due to economic depression

    d. retirees

12. Workers that are released from employment for temporary periods of time and brought back to the same jobs are said to be

    a. retired.

    b. laid off.

    c. fired.

    d. underemployed.

13. The federal government borrows money by

    a. delaying payments to employees.

    b. selling bonds.

    c. cutting off funding to certain programs.

    d. taxing citizens and corporations.

14. The federal government regulates

    a. gubernatorial elections.

    b. school curricula.

    c. state universities.

    d. interstate commerce.

15. The federal government can print more money to stimulate the economy, however this may cause

    a. deflation.

    b. stagflation.

    c. inflation.

    d. unemployment.

16. Classical economics holds that over time, economic problems will be corrected by the

    a. policies of the government.

    b. invisible hand of the market.

    c. people.

    d. raising of taxes.

17. A lack of money to fund a budget is called a

    a. deficit.

    b. savings.

    c. debt.

    d. loan

18. The federal government has carried significant amounts of debt since

    a. the Civil War.

    b. the 1980s.

    c. the Great Depression.

    d. the 2010s.

19. The value of all goods and services produced in a country is the

    a. per Capita Income.

    b. gross Domestic Product.

    c. net Exports.

    d. capital.

20. When a country chooses to spend time and resources making a product, it loses out on all of the other products it could have spent its time and resources making. This is known as

   a. a deficit.
   b. opportunity cost.
   c. economy of scale.
   d. gross domestic income.

Part VI - Social Studies Skills and Concepts

1. What is the established way groups of people look at philosophical views and religious faith called?

   a, Conflict
   b. Belief Systems
   c. Change
   d. Culture

2. Relying on others in mutually beneficial ways is known as _____.

   a. Interdependence
   b. Empathy
   c. Identity
   d. Choice

3. Individuals given fair treatment in personal, societal, and governmental interactions is called _____.

   a. Power
   b. Empathy
   c. Justice
   d. Citizenship

4. The basic political, social, and economic rights that all humans are entitled to are known as:

    a. Laws
    b. Human Rights
    c. Justice
    d. Values

5. The principles that serve as the foundation for the United States' form of government are called _____.

    a. Justice
    b. Citizenship
    c. Civic Values
    d. Decision Making

6. What is the process we use to influence the many facets of our lives?

    a. Decision Making
    b. Rule Breaking
    c. Rationalizing
    d. Diversifying

7. A politically organized society is run by a _____.

    a. Dictatorship
    b. Oligarchy
    c. Monarchy
    jd. Government

8. Your ability to influence the actions of others refers to your _____.

    a. Citizenship
    b. Power
    c. Influence
    d. Empathy

9. Monarchies, oligarchies, dictatorships, democracies, republics, etc. are all _____.

    a. Political Systems

    b. Negative governments

    c. Positive governments

    d. Effective governments

10. Voting fulfills one of the responsibilities of _____ in the United States.

    a. Justice

    b. Rights

    c. Citizenship

    d. Ruling

11. People who are united by a geographic location or by a political organization are a part of the same _____-state.

    a. Dictatorial

    b. Democratic

    c. Republican

    d. Nation

12. The conflict between our unlimited needs and wants and how many human and natural resources there are to fulfill them is called _____.

    a. Scarcity

    b. Depletion

    c. Destruction

    d. Expenditure

13. _____ is defined as the natural and manmade elements that surround us.

    a. Location
    b. Environment
    c. Geography
    d. Social Studies

14. The study of human activity on earth, including the way human settlement impacts Earth's surface, is called _____.

    a. Human Systems
    b., Human Studies
    c. Globalism
    d. Global Systems

15. _____ systems are the processes that shape Earth's surface. It includes the interaction of plant and animal life.

    Geography
    Human
    Physical
    Ecology

Answer Key

Part 1 - History

1. B
Combining copper and tin creates bronze.

Choice A is incorrect; there is no Tin Age.

Choice C is incorrect; The Stone Age came before The Bronze Age and is known for its use of stone, not metal.

Choice D is incorrect; The Iron Age came after The Bronze Age and is known for its use of iron.

2. A
The Punic Wars happened in Rome in the 3rd century BCE.

Choice B is incorrect; the Persian Wars happened in the 5th century BCE.

Choice C is incorrect; the Parthenon was constructed during the 5th century BCE.

Choice D is incorrect; Socrates lived in Greece during the 5th century BCE.

3. D
Democracy was first introduced in Athens in the 6th century.

Choice A is incorrect; dictatorships were first introduced in Rome in the 6th century.

Choice B is incorrect; Communism was first introduced in Russia in the 19th century.

Choice C is incorrect; Capitalism was first introduced in Europe in the MIddle Ages.

4. A
Ares, Aphrodite, Demeter and Athena are the names of four ancient Greek gods.

Choice B is incorrect; when Rome overtook Greece, they adopted some of their gods, but called them by different names.

Choices C is incorrect, Egyptian and Norse gods had different names.

5. C
Egypt attacking Rome at that time did not contribute to the fall of the Roman Empire. All the other choice were contributing factors.

Choice A is incorrect; the spread of Christianity displaced Roman religion.

Choice B is incorrect; Rome had grown very large and difficult to govern leading to civil war.

Choice D is incorrect; as Rome stopped expanding they were no longer gaining slaves and were unable to support themselves.

6. D
Vedas are ancient texts composed in Vedic Sandskrit.

Choice A is incorrect; this was not a time period in history.

Choice B is incorrect; this was not the name of the ruling class.

Choice C is incorrect; it is not known what happened to the Harappans, and the next invaders were the Aryans.

7. A
There is some doubt as to whether the Xia Dynasty existed, however, some recorded and archeological evidence that hints that it did.

Choice B is incorrect; the Han dynasty was a golden age in

Chinese history where Imperial China started, but it was not the first dynasty.

Choice C is incorrect; the Tang dynasty is another golden age of culture and society of Chinese history, Chang'an the capital of China was the largest city in the world at the time.

Choice D is incorrect; the Qing Dynasty was the last imperial dynasty of China, not the first.

8. D
Both Isaac Newton and Gottfried Leibniz discovered calculus independently - it was not invented by the Chinese.

The other choices are all inventions by the Chinese. Paper making was invented by the Chinese around 200 BCE, the Chinese first used chemical warfare during about 400 BCE, using the smoke of burnt mustard plants to kill their enemies, and the first use of gunpowder by the Chinese was before 1000 CE.

9. A
Buddhism maintains anyone can follow the Eightfold path to correct behavior and reach Nirvana.

Choice B is incorrect; in Hinduism, someone must go through a series of reincarnations before they can reach enlightenment.

Choice C is incorrect; Islam follows the teachings of the Qur'an.

Choice D is incorrect; Taoism is a Chinese philosophy of living.

10. B
Islam emerged in Arabia in 7th century CE. Some archaeologists prefer to use the terms Before the Common Era (B.C.E.) and the Common Era (C.E.), which are exactly the same as B.C. and A.D. but have nothing to do with Christianity.

Choice A is incorrect; Christianity emerged in Rome in 1st

century CE.

Choice C is incorrect; Judaism emerged in Israel in 6th century BCE.

Choice D is incorrect; Zoroastrianism emerged in Indo-Iran in 2nd century BCE.

11. B
A national language is not necessary to form a Nation.

Choice A is incorrect; breaking with the Catholic Church gave more power to the monarchy and increased nationalism in England.

Choice C is incorrect; Napoleon was influential in unifying France and caused other European nations to band together.

Choice D is incorrect; the creation of central governments caused laws and policy to be uniform across nations.

12. D
Following the fall of the Roman Empire, the Roman army was no longer supported by tax from the elite. Had this tax continued to support the Roman army, they could have stopped the inward migration.

Choice A is incorrect; Eastern Europe did not experience violence during this time.

Choice B is incorrect; rapid increases in population did not cause large scale migration.

Choice C is incorrect; the Roman Empire was not experiencing prosperity at that time.

13. C
The printing press is generally thought to be the most important invention of the Renaissance, and perhaps in the history of the world. Invented by German Johannes Gutenberg around 1440, the printing press made classical texts and other works available on a large scale, which influenced Renaissance thinking. By 1500 there were printing presses

throughout Europe.

Choice A is incorrect; the steam engine was developed during the Industrial Revolution.

Choice B is incorrect; the flying shuttle was developed during the Industrial Revolution.

Choice D is incorrect; although lenses were developed during the Renaissance, they were not a cause.

14. A
Thomas More was a Renaissance humanist who wrote about the Utopian political system in Utopia.

Choice B is incorrect; Niccolo Machiavelli was a Renaissance writer who wrote The Prince.

Choice C is incorrect; Martin Luther was a Renaissance Protestant leader who wrote the 95 theses attacking the Church.

Choice D is incorrect; Nicholas Copernicus was a Renaissance mathematician who developed the heliocentric view of the universe.

15. C
Although people increasingly looked to the monarchy to solve their problems, this was not a result of the Renaissance.

Choice A is incorrect; during the Renaissance the arts and sciences flourished.

Choice B is incorrect; the Church no longer possessed the unquestioned authority that it once had.

Choice D is incorrect; there was increased use of national languages such as English, Italian, and French.

16. B
An increased spirit of inquiry by the people, interference by the Pope in non-religious matters and selling of indulgences

by the Church led to the Reformation, which was a loss of power for the Church and Pope.

Choice A is incorrect; the Renaissance was a time of intellectual growth before the Reformation.

Choice C is incorrect; the Scientific Revolution was a time of advancement in the sciences following Reformation.

Choice D is incorrect; the Protestant Revolution was a Puritan rebellion in Maryland, though the Reformation is sometimes called the Protestant Reformation.

17. D
Following the Reformation, there was an increase in religious prosecution through the Spanish Inquisition, not an end to religious persecution.

Choice A is incorrect; Protestantism was formed during the Reformation.

Choice B is incorrect; The Thirty Years' War was a conflict between Catholics and Protestants following Reformation.

Choice C is incorrect; rulers had more power following the Reformation and did not need to listen to the Pope.

18. C
Martin Luther is most famous for pinning his 95 theses to a church door, which started the Reformation.

Choice A is incorrect; John Calvin's writings led to the formation of Presbyterian churches.

Choice B is incorrect; Martin Luther was not a priest and did not promote religious tolerance.

Choice D is incorrect; Thomas More wrote Utopia.

19. A
Johannes Kepler wrote the laws of planetary motion, which later influenced Isaac Newton.

Choice B is incorrect; Galileo was a scientist who invented the microscope and telescope.

Choice C is incorrect; Francis Bacon studied logic and ethics in science.

Choice D is incorrect; Rene Descartes was the inventor of deductive reasoning.

20. A
Nicholas Copernicus determined that the earth revolves around the sun.

Choice B is incorrect; Tycho Brahe believed that the sun moved around the earth and other planets moved around the sun.

Choice C is incorrect; Francis Bacon studied logic and ethics in science.

Choice D is incorrect; Isaac Newton studied universal laws of gravitation.

Part II - US History

1. D
The Foreign Trade Act did not take place until centuries after the American Revolutionary War. All the Intolerable Acts took place in the lead-up to the American Revolutionary War.

Choice A is incorrect; the Stamp Act imposed a tax on the colonies by forcing them to use paper produced in Britain for many printed materials. This was the first of the Intolerable Acts or taxes that were placed on British American subjects without their consent.

Choice B is incorrect; the Townshed Acts were also part of the Intolerable Acts that were meant to raise revenue in the colonies for the employment of judges and governors.

These were also used to punish colonists and force compliance with the numerous other taxes being levied against the colonies.

Choice C is incorrect; the Tea Act allowed the British East India Company to sell tea directly to the colonies, thus making it cheaper. Many colonists hated this act because a small tax was added without their consent, which resulted in the Boston Tea Party.

2. B
The British imposed taxes through the Intolerable Acts either without representation from the colonies at all, or with representatives that effectively had no say in the matter.

Choice A is incorrect; even during the American Revolutionary War, most of the colonists did not decisively want to be free from British rule; they either wanted to stay under British rule, or were undecided.

Choice C is incorrect; while Colonists and people everywhere do not like to be taxed, most realized taxes were what allowed government to function and the colonists made no statements against ALL taxes, just some of them.

3. B
After the Seven Years War with France, Great Britain had a lot of debt and Parliament wanted the colonies to pay for some of the military expenditures and the cost of maintaining a military presence in the colonies.

Choice A is incorrect; None of the Intolerable Acts were used to raise revenue for the British Parliament salaries. The Intolerable Acts were used to pay off war debt, punish the colonies, and a variety of other things.

Choice C is incorrect; the Navigation Acts kept most trade in the British Colonies strictly between the colonies and Great Britain.

Choice D is incorrect; while the East India Company was fighting in India at this time, the British military was not involved there yet.

4. A
The Second Continental Congress tried to avert war even though the battles of Lexington and Concord had already been fought. This was known as the Olive Branch Petition. King James would not receive the petition because it came from what he perceived as an illegal and illegitimate assembly.

Choice C is false; because while Thomas Jefferson wrote the first draft of the petition, most of it was redrafted, and it was never called Jefferson's Plea.

Choice D is false; neither Samuel nor John Adams thought the Plea would help, and contributed nothing to the process. The plea was never called Adam's Plea.

5. A
The First continental Congress met to discuss various ways of getting rid of the Intolerable Acts and petition the King of England for a redress of grievances.

Choice B is incorrect; this is the purpose of the Second Continental Congress.

Choice C is incorrect; the federal government was set up with the Articles of Confederation.

Choice D is incorrect; all the "states" at this point were not states yet, instead they were colonies that firmly belonged to Great Britain.

6. D
While many other things were achieved, the main purpose of the Second Continental Congress was to establish a Continental Army.

Choice A is incorrect; the federal government was set up with the Articles of Confederation

Choice B is incorrect; Responding to the Intolerable Acts was the purpose of the First Continental Congress

Choice C is incorrect; asking for French aid was officially

done after the Second Continental Congress was over, though Benjamin Franklin and others hinted at this possibility with many French officials.

7. B
With the Declaration of Independence, the colonies disavowed the rule of Great Britain, effectively announcing a state of war between the colonists and Great Britain.

Choice A is incorrect; the Articles of Confederation Established a federal government and occurred after there was a state of war between Great Britain and the Colonies.

Choice C is incorrect; the United States Constitution was a document that strengthened the federal government and, provided more effective ways of raising revenue.

Choice C is incorrect; while a declaration of hostilities does announce a state of war, there was no such document called the Declaration of Hostilities.

8. D
All the reasons listed were part of Manifest Destiny,

- Many Americans believed that they were special and could use the land better than anyone else.

- The agrarian ideal was a very popular idea at the time, many dreamed that America should be populated by self-sufficient farmers. With all the "open" land in the west this seemed like a real possibility.

- Many Americans believed that God had set America a destiny to bring civilization to the west, and that America would one day stretch across the continent.

9. A
The Clermont steamboat's maiden voyage between New York and Albany took 32 hours, much less time than the four days it would take the average sloop. This showed that distances between areas were shrinking time-wise.

Choice B is incorrect; while the Mexican American War brought many people west it was not the start of western expansion.

Choice C is incorrect; the invention of the telegraph greatly helped communication across the country, but it was not invented until long after western expansion had started.

Choice D is incorrect; gold in California brought more people west faster than ever before, but western expansion had already started decades before.

10. B
Gold was discovered in California in 1848, and the Gold Rush commenced.

Choice A is incorrect; while the miners were called 49ers after the year that most people started mining for gold in California, this was not when the Gold Rush started.

Choice C is incorrect; this was the year that the Gold Rush ended in California.

Choice D is incorrect; this was the year that California was admitted to the Union, not when the Gold Rush started.

11. A
The largest land acquisition, The Louisiana Purchase, was orchestrated under the Jefferson Administration and nearly doubled the size of the United States adding on almost 828,000 square miles.

Choice B is incorrect; the Treaty of Guadalupe Hidalgo added 525,000 sq miles to the United States and Mexico lost nearly half of their land. This was still a smaller land acquisition than the Louisiana Purchase.

Choice C is incorrect; the Texas Annexation incorporated the Republic of Texas into the United States and brought in about 390,000 square miles of land to the Union. This was also less than the Louisiana Purchase.

Choice D is incorrect; the Gadsden Purchase was the last time that the United States acquired land from Mexico with this $10 million purchase which added territory onto New Mexico and Arizona. This acquisition was for about 30,000 sqare miles which was less than the Louisiana Purchase.

12. D
Texas was an independent nation from about 1836 to 1845 with its own government and president. Mexico did not recognize its independence, but they were effectively independent until annexation by the United States in 1845.

Choice A is incorrect; Delaware was the first state in the Union in 1787, but was not created during westward expansion. Before being a state, it was a colony of Great Britain, not a sovereign nation.

Choice B is incorrect; California claimed to be an independent nation for less than a year, but never installed a civil administration or a president.

Choice C is incorrect; Alaska was a territory of Russia before becoming part of the Union, and never was a sovereign nation.

13. C
The Transcontinental Railroad greatly reduced the time it took to travel across the United States from almost half a year to about a week.

Choice A is incorrect; the telegraph was the fastest way for information (not people) to travel across the Continental United States.

Choice B is incorrect; the Clearmont steamboat marked the start of westward expansion, but it did not provide the shortest trip across the United States.

Choice D is incorrect; the Northwest Passage is a sea route that runs through the Arctic Ocean from the tips of Russia and Alaska, above Canada, and into the Atlantic Ocean. It was first discovered in 1903, but remained closed for most of each year until about 2010. This passage was dangerous and never a significant part of western expansion.

14. A
With Arizona's statehood in 1912, all the west to the Pacific ocean was incorporated into the United States.

Choice B is incorrect; the end of the Mexican American War in 1848 was more than half a century before the end of western expansion.

Choice C is incorrect; there is no such thing as the Completion Speech.

Choice D is incorrect; President William Mckinley's Assassination in 1901 did not have an effect on westward expansion.

15. C
Many Native Americans were forcefully relocated out of the Deep South if they failed to assimilate. This occurred during much of the 1830s. Most deaths occurred near the end when the army detained many Native Americans who had not left and forced them west, many died due to disease, exposure and starvation.

Choice A is incorrect; the Trail of Tears occurred before the United States military and the various Sioux tribes were at war.

Choice B is incorrect; Irish immigrants were never forcefully removed en mass from New York

Choice D is incorrect; while the Transcontinental Railroad claimed many lives in its construction no part of it was ever called the Trail of Tears.

16. A
Democrat President Jackson and his supporters believed that all white males, the common man, should have the right to vote, and not just those that owned property or paid certain taxes.

Choice B is incorrect; almost no one believed minorities should be able to vote.

Choice C is incorrect; women were not directly part of the political process and the belief that women were too "fragile" or emotional for the process would hold sway after the Jacksonian Democrats were no longer a political party.

Choice D is incorrect; Jacksonian Democrats were explicitly against the landed gentry having all the political power.

17. C

The Second Great Awakening was a movement that rejected skepticism and rationalism. The supporters called for everyone to become more moral and less analytical.

Choice A is incorrect; while it was a multi-denominational religious movement, people believed the second coming of Christ was imminent, which would be followed by a thousand years of peace, not the end of the world.

Choice B is incorrect; the Second Great Awakening was a religious movement that emphasized faith over logic.

Choice D is incorrect; while reducing corruption in politics may have been part of the increase in morality the Second Great Awakening called for, the movement was religious, and not about corruption in politics.

18. B

With Marbury v. Madison, Chief Justice Marshall allowed Marshall to establish the concept of judicial review. Judicial review is the concept that only the supreme court can declare a law unconstitutional, and is the sole power of the Supreme Court.

Choice A is incorrect; Fletcher v. Peck in 1810 was the first ruling that ruled a state law was unconstitutional. This enlarged the powers of the supreme court, but not as much as Marbury v. Madison.

Choice C is incorrect; Brown vs. Board of Education declared that segregated schools were unconstitutional. The ruling had no effect on the powers of the Supreme Court and was not presided over by Chief Justice Marshall.

Choice D is incorrect; Roe vs. Wade dealt with when women

could get abortions. This did not have an effect on the Supreme Court's power, nor did Chief Justice Marshall preside over the court that decided that case.

19. D
While the Lewis and Clark expedition did try to establish some American presence in unclaimed territory on the West Coast, they did not try to claim any of the Spanish territory on the border of the Louisiana Purchase.

Choice A is incorrect; exploring and mapping the Louisiana Purchase was a chief reason that the expedition was funded.

Choice B is incorrect; President Jefferson's main purpose for the expedition was to find a water route across the continent for future commerce.

Choice C is incorrect; the United States did want to establish a presence in the Louisiana Territory to strengthen their claim.

20. B
The First Barbary War was the first war on a foreign soil authorized by congress.

Choice A is incorrect; many European powers paid tribute to the Barbary States to ensure that their trading ships were not harassed.

Choice C is incorrect; Spain suggested the United States should pay the tribute to prevent further attacks after the Spanish negotiated for the release of the captured ship and crew.

Choice D is incorrect; while the United States was winning some strategic battles, a treaty was drawn up in which there would be an end to hostilities and a complete prisoner exchange, with the United States paying an additional ransom for the extra prisoners Tripoli had.

Part III - Geography

1. C
Open spaces is not a reason that humans move to urban areas.

Choice A is incorrect; people move to cities for excitement.

Choice B is incorrect; most universities are located in cities.

Choice D is incorrect; cities normally have more job opportunities than rural areas.

2. B
The era of human existence before writing was developed is known as prehistory.

Choices A and B are incorrect; ancient and recorded history are written.

Choice D is incorrect; unknown history is not a real term.

3. C
A thin stretch of land that connects two large areas of land is called an isthmus.

4. B
An ecosystem is a group of living organisms and their surrounding environment.

All the other choices are incorrect, but plausible, due to the eco- prefix.

5. B
The Indian ocean borders the east coast of Africa.

Choice A is incorrect; the Atlantic borders the west coast.

Choices C and D are clearly incorrect; the pacific doesn't border Africa.

6. A
Cuba, Haiti and Puerto Rico are located in the Caribbean Sea.

Choice B is incorrect; the North Sea borders Europe.

Choice C is incorrect; the Indian Ocean borders Asia and Africa.

Choice D is incorrect; the Black Sea is adjacent to the Mediterranean.

7. D
The Ural Mountains separate the continents of Europe and Asia.
Choice A is incorrect; North and South America are not separated by mountains.

Choice B is incorrect; Africa and Asia are not separated by mountains.

Choice C is incorrect; Australia is an island.

8. A
Australia is a contintent, though not a large one.

Continents have the following characteristics:

- Areas of geologically stable continental crust, or cratons, tectonically independent from other continents
- Biological distinctiveness, with unique animal and plant life
- Cultural uniqueness
- Local belief in separate continental status

9. A
A nation is also known as a country; nation and country are interchangeable terms.

Choice B is incorrect; although nations have governments, they are not interchangeable.

Choice C is incorrect; a society does not have to be a nation.

Choice D is clearly incorrect; a utopia is a fictional place.

10. D
Physical maps show features such as mountains, lakes and rivers.

Choice A is incorrect; a political map shows borders of countries.

Choice B is incorrect; movements of populations are not shown on a physical map.

Choice C is incorrect; ruins are not shown on a physical map.

11. A
Country borders are a feature shown most clearly on a political map.

Choice B is incorrect; movements of populations are not shown on a political map.

Choice C is incorrect; ruins are not shown on a political map.

Choice D is incorrect; a physical map shows features such as mountains, lakes and rivers.

12. C
Anthropology is the study of human movements and the development of society.

Choice A is incorrect; biology is the study of organic life.

Choice B is incorrect; archeology is the study of artifacts.

Choice D is incorrect; paleontology is the study of fossils.

13. B
The study of the artifacts is known as archaeology.

Choice A is incorrect; biology is the study of how life works.

Choice C is incorrect; anthropology is the study of human movements and the development of society.

Choice D is incorrect; paleontology is the study of fossils.

14. D
The connection of different societies through technology such as the telephone, cellular phone and internet is known as the communications revolution.

Choice A and C are incorrect; agriculture has little to do with this.

Choice B is incorrect; the industrial revolution came earlier.

15. B
Globalization refers to the connection of all the economies in the world.

Choice A is incorrect; globalization refers to economics, not education.

Choice C is incorrect; although plausible due to the large colonial territories it refers to.

Choice D is incorrect; the study of ancient civilizations is archeology.

16. A
A brief definition of Geography is the study of lands, features and phenomena of the Earth.

The full definition is, the study of the physical features of the earth and its atmosphere, and of human activity as it affects and is affected by these, including the distribution of populations and resources, land use, and industries.
All the other choices omit one or more parts of the definition.

17. B
Area studies are the study of human-land relationships

18. A
The two branches of Geography are, human geography and physical geography.

19. A
Environmental geography is the interactions between the environment and humans.

Choice B, a combination of physical and human geography, is a good answer, but choice A is the best choice.

20. C
Geomorphology is the scientific study of the origin and evolution of topographic and bathymetric features created by physical or chemical processes operating at, or near Earth's surface.

Part IV - Civics and Government

1. A
A political system with a king or queen as leader is a monarchy.

Choices B and C are incorrect by definition, it would need to be "republican monarchy" or "constitutional monarchy" to be closer to the correct answer.

Choice D is clearly incorrect, since Utopia is a fictional place

2. C
The concept of voting dates back to ancient civilization.

Choices A is incorrect because voting existed before the Enlightenment.

Choice B is incorrect because voting existed before the American Revolution.

Choice D is incorrect because voting existed before the Renaissance.

3. D
Dictatorships have strong leaders and the people have virtually no power.

Choice A is partly correct as dictatorships have strong leaders, but the leader is not held responsible to the will of the people.

Choice B is incorrect; dictatorships normally only have one political party. The answer is a good definition of a republic.

Choice C is incorrect because in a dictatorship, virtually no power rests with the people.

4. B
Choice A is incorrect because nationalism is similar to patriotism.

Choice C is incorrect because justice is about punishing criminals, although selecting this answer does show some good thinking.

Choice D is incorrect because liberty is irrelevant to the question.

5. D
A plutocracy is a country or society governed by the wealthy.

6. D
The ancient Romans had a legislative branch of government known as the Senate.

Choice A is incorrect because the Roman Emperor was not the legislative branch.

Choice B is incorrect because a president not a legislator and the term "president" was not used in ancient Roman government.

Choice C is incorrect because a court is not a legislative branch.

7. A
A government controlled by elected representatives is known as a Republic.

Choice B is incorrect; since a Utopia is a fictional place.

Choice C is incorrect by definition; it would need to be "constitutional monarchy" to be closer to a correct answer.

8. D
The primary purpose of the Magna Carta was to take power from the king and give it to Parliament.

Choice A is incorrect; it had little to do with the peasants.

Choice B is incorrect; it took power from the king and gave it to Parliament.

Choice C is incorrect; it had little to do with the military.

9. D
A theocracy is a government controlled by religious leaders based on adherence to a religion.

Choices A and B are incorrect by definition.

Choice C is clearly incorrect because anarchy refers to a lack of government.

10. A
A constitution a document that outlines the principles and structure of a government.

Choice B is the definition of a subpoena.

Choice C is the definition of a petition.

Choice D is the definition of the Emancipation Proclamation.

11. B
A confederation is an organization that consists of a number of parties or groups united in an alliance or league.

Choice A is incorrect since a confederation does not have a strong central government.

Choice C is incorrect since a dictatorship is a strong central government.

Choice D is incorrect since a theocracy is based on religion.

12. B
Claiming land is not mentioned in the Constitution as a purpose for government.

Choices A, C and D are incorrect since to form a more perfect union, provide for the common defense, and establishing justice are all listed in the preamble.

13. D
Karl Marx wrote that most struggles are between, the haves and have-nots, the rich and poor, etc.

Choices A, B and C may sound like a plausible answers to someone unfamiliar with Marx.

14. B
Democracy is the most common form of government.

Choice A is incorrect; most countries do not have a king or queen.

Choice C is incorrect; although there were many autocracies in the past.

Choice D is incorrect because there are very few dictatorships left.

15. A
Nebraska was not part of the original thirteen colonies, which should be clear from Nebraska's geographical location if not from simply knowing the 13 colonies from memory. Choice B is incorrect; Virginia was one of the most important colonies.

Choice C is incorrect; Georgia was the southernmost of the

13 colonies.

Choice D is incorrect; New York was one of the 13 colonies.

16. A
At the time of the American Revolution, the English government was a constitutional monarchy.

Choice B is incorrect because the government was not controlled by religious leaders.

Choice C is incorrect because dictatorships came later and are distinct from monarchies.

Choice D is incorrect because the king was not elected.

17. B
The question asks which of the choices were not a cause of the American Revolution. The institution of slavery is the only choice that was not a cause of the American Revolution.

Choice B is correct; slavery was common in the colonies and was not a point of contention.

The other choices are all incorrect, Enlightenment philosophy was a cause, taxes were a cause and the Boston Massacre was a cause.

18. A
For hundreds of years, England has had a legislative branch of government known as Parliament.

Choice B is incorrect; Congress is the name of the American legislature.

Choice C is incorrect; the Senate is one of the U.S. houses of congress.

Choice D is clearly incorrect because courts are not legislative in nature.

19. D
The Declaration of Independence lists universal rights as life,

liberty, the pursuit of happiness are the "inalienable" rights.

Choices A, B and C are incorrect as education and health, literacy and wealth are not mentioned in the Declaration of Independence.

20. A
The first ten amendments to the U.S. Constitution are also known as the Bill of Rights.

Choice B is incorrect since the Declaration of the Rights of Man was an earlier document.

Choice C is incorrect; the Human Rights Act came much later.

Choice D is incorrect; the Declaration of Independence was an earlier document.

Part V - Economics

1. A
As demand increases, supply tends to decrease.

Choice B is incorrect; supply and demand tend to be inversely related.

Choice C is clearly incorrect; demand has a strong influence on supply.

Choice D is incorrect; demand has a predictable effect on supply.

2. B
As supply increases, prices tend to decrease.

Choice A is incorrect; more supply lowers prices

Choices C and D are incorrect; supply has a predictable effect on prices.

3. A

As economies of scale increase, products are expensive to make at first, but eventually become less expensive to make. This usually applies to large items, such as airplanes and cars.

Choice B is incorrect; the opposite is true.

Choice C is incorrect; here products are not customized to individual customers.

Choice D is incorrect; bidding is irrelevant to production.

4. C

In a free market economy, citizens own resources and private property.

Choices A and D are incorrect by definition.

Choice B is the definition of a command economy.

5. B

In a command economy, the government owns the resources and does not allow citizens to own private property.

Choices A and D are incorrect by definition.

Choice C is incorrect; this is the definition of a free market economy.

6. C

Capital is the resource (namely money) needed to start or expand a business.

Choice A is incorrect; per capita income is a measure of individual income.

Choices B and D are incorrect but may sound plausible.

7. C

An increase in the value of money, or more precisely, a general increase in prices and fall in the purchasing value of money.

Choice A is incorrect; inflation refers to currency, not business.

Choice B is incorrect; this is the definition of deflation.

Choice D is incorrect; unemployment is not a cause of inflation.

8. D
A country's labor force excludes children who are too young to work and are not calculated as part of the job market.

Choice A is incorrect; professionals are included.

Choices B and C are incorrect but the word "labor" makes them seem plausible.

9. A
A miner is a physical laborer and a good example of a blue collar occupation.

Choices B, C and D are incorrect; a professor, a scientist and an accountant are all professionals.

10. A
Consumer confidence is an economic indicator which measures the degree of optimism consumers feel about the overall state of the economy and their personal financial situation.

Choices B and C are incorrect but sound plausible.

11. D
Unemployment figures do not include retirees, who are not expected to work.

Choice A is incorrect; white collar workers are an important part of unemployment statistics.

Choice B is incorrect; government employees are an important part of unemployment statistics.

Choice C is incorrect; economic depression affects unemployment figures greatly.

12. B
Workers that are released from employment for temporary periods of time and brought back to the same jobs are said to be laid off.

Choice A is incorrect; retired people are not expected to return to work.

Choice C is incorrect; fired workers do not expect to return to the same position.

Choice D is incorrect; underemployed workers simply want more hours to work.

13. B
The federal government borrows money by selling bonds. Bonds are loans to the government by the bond-holders.

Choices A and C are incorrect; delaying payments to employees, or cutting off funding do not amount to borrowing money.

Choice D is incorrect; taxing citizens and corporations is how the government gets its revenue.

14. D
The federal government regulates interstate commerce.

Choices A, B and C are incorrect; gubernatorial elections, school curricula, and state universities are a state and local matter.

15. C
The federal government can print money to stimulate the economy, however, increasing the money supply decreases the value of money and causes inflation.

Choice A is incorrect; deflation is an increase in the value of money.

Choice B is incorrect; stagflation is a possibility, but does not normally take place.

Choice D is incorrect; stagnation is a stalling of the economy, while increasing the money supply stimulates the economy.

16. B
Classical economics holds that over time, economic problems will be corrected by the invisible hand of the market. Adam Smith's theory of the invisible hand is an important part of classical economics.

Choice A is incorrect; classical economics was a free market school of thought.

Choice C is incorrect; the people's role in classical economics is simply to be consumers of goods produced.

Choice D is incorrect; classical economists would virtually never recommend raising taxes.

17. A
A lack of money to fund a budget is called a deficit.

Choice B is incorrect; a lack of money does not amount to a savings.

Choices C and D are incorrect; a debt, or a loan is money borrowed to cover deficits.

18. B
The federal government has carried significant amounts of debt since the 1980s, when it became normal for the U.S. to borrow more and more money each year to cover deficits.

Choice A is incorrect; the Civil War required borrowing, but the debts were not carried for long and paid off.

Choice C is incorrect; the Great Depression created debt, but the debts were paid off by the end of the 1940s.

Choice D is incorrect; 2010 was not the beginning of the practice of carrying large amounts of debt.

19. B
The value of all goods and services produced within a country is the Gross Domestic Product, or GDP.

Choice A is incorrect; per capita income is a measure of individual income.

Choice C is incorrect; net exports are only part of GDP.

Choice D is incorrect; capital is money and resources used to expand a business.

20. B
When a country chooses to spend time and resources making a product, it loses out on all the other products it could have spent its time and resources making. This is known as opportunity cost.

Choice A is incorrect; a deficit is a budget shortage.

Choice C is incorrect; an economy of scale is not particularly related to opportunity cost.

Choice D is incorrect; gross domestic income is the total income brought into the economy.

Part VI - Social Studies Skills and Concepts

1. B
Belief systems are the established ways groups of people look at philosophical views and religious faith.

Choice A is incorrect. Conflict is a clash of ideas from incompatible forces.

Choice C is incorrect. Change is trying to evoke an alteration in ideas or events.

Choice D is incorrect. Culture is patterns of human

behavior (ideas, beliefs, values, etc.) that are transmitted to succeeding generations.

2. A
Interdependence is defined as relying on others in mutually beneficial ways.

Choice B is incorrect. Empathy is your ability to understand others because you're able to share their feelings.

Choice C is incorrect. Identity is your own unique values and attitudes.

Choice D is incorrect. Choice is your right to select from many alternatives

3. C
Justice is upheld when individuals are given fair treatment in personal, societal, and governmental interactions.

Choice A is incorrect; Power is your ability to influence the actions of others.

Choice B is incorrect; Empathy is your ability to understand others because you're able to share their feelings.

Choice D is incorrect; Citizenship happens when a country gives a person a recognized status under the law

4. B
Human rights are the basic political, social, and economic rights that all human are entitled to.

Choice A is incorrect; Laws are the rules governing the region you are in.

Choice C is incorrect; Justice happens when individuals are given fair treatment in personal, societal, and governmental interactions.

Choice D is incorrect; Values are the principles by which you live your life.

5. C
Civic Values are the principles that serve as the foundation for the United States' form of government.

Choice A is incorrect; Justice happens when individuals are given fair treatment in personal, societal, and governmental interactions.

Choice B is incorrect; Citizenship happens when a country gives a person a recognized status under the law.

Choice D is incorrect; Decision Making is that process that we use to influence the many facets of our lives.

6. A
Decision Making is that process that we use to influence the many facets of our lives.

Choice B is incorrect; Rule breaking is not an official term, but refers to the time when a person breaks a rule or law.

Choice C is incorrect; Rationalizing is not an official term, but refers to the idea of a person trying to justify their actions by equating them with actions that are more acceptable.

Choice D is incorrect; Diversifying is an economic term used to describe a portfolio that is invested in many areas.

7. D
A politically organized society is run by a government.

Choice A is incorrect; A dictatorship is a form of government run by the absolute authority of a dictator.

Choice B is incorrect; An oligarchy is form of government run by a small group of people.

Choice C is incorrect; A monarchy is a form of government where sovereignty is embodied in one person.

8. B
Power is your ability to influence the actions of others.

Choice A is incorrect; Citizenship happens when a country gives a person a recognized status under the law.

Choice C is incorrect; Influence is similar to power, but it focuses more on character rather than actions.

Choice D is incorrect; Empathy is your ability to understand others because you're able to share their feelings.

9. A
Monarchies, oligarchies, dictatorships, democracies, and republics are all political systems.

Choice B is incorrect; Though some forms of government are perceived as negative, all of them are not.

Choice C is incorrect; Though some forms of government are perceived as positive, all of them are not.

Choice D is incorrect; Though some forms of government are perceived as effective, all of them are not.

10. C
Voting fulfills one of the responsibility of citizenship.

Choice A is incorrect; Justice happens when individuals are given fair treatment in personal, societal, and governmental interactions.

Choice B is incorrect; Rights are the legal principles of freedom for individuals.

Choice D is incorrect; Voting does not allow people to rule the United States.

11. D
People are united by a geographic location or by a political organization are a part of the same nation-sate.

Choice A is incorrect; A dictatorial state is run by a dictator.

Choice B is incorrect; A democratic state is governed by the people.

Choice C is incorrect; A republican state is ruled by elected leaders, where the power resides in the people.

12. A
The conflict between our unlimited needs and how many natural resources there are is called scarcity.

Choice B is incorrect; Depletion is the reduction in the quantity of a certain thing.

Choice C is incorrect; Destruction is the act of causing damage to something so that it no longer exists.

Choice D is incorrect; Expenditure is the act of spending.

13. B
An environment is defined as the natural and manmade elements that surround us.

Choice A is incorrect; A location is simply a place.

Choice C is incorrect; Geography is the study of the earth's surface.

Choice D is incorrect; Social Studies is the study of history, geography, economics, government, etc.

14. A
The study of human activity on earth is called Human Systems.

Choice B is incorrect; The study of human activity on earth is called Human Systems.

Choice C is incorrect; Globalism is the attitude that places the interests of the world over those of individual countries.

Choice D is incorrect; The study of human activity on earth is called Human Systems.

15. C
Physical systems are the processes that shape Earth's surface.

Choice A is incorrect; Geography is the study of the earth's surface.

Choice B is incorrect; The study of human activity on earth is called Human Systems.

Choice D is incorrect; Ecology is a branch of biology that focuses on the relationships of organisms to their surroundings.

Practice Test Questions Set 2

The questions below are not the same as you will find on the WEST-E® Social Studies test- that would be too easy! And nobody knows what the questions will be and they change all the time. Below are general questions that cover the same subject areas as the WEST-E® Social Studies test. So, while the format and exact wording of the questions may differ slightly, and change from year to year, if you can answer the questions below, you will have no problem with the WEST-E® Social Studies test.

For the best results, take these Practice Test Questions as if it were the real exam. Set aside time when you will not be disturbed, and a location that is quiet and free of distractions. Read the instructions carefully, read each question carefully, and answer to the best of your ability.
Use the bubble answer sheets provided. When you have completed the Practice Questions, check your answer against the Answer Key and read the explanation provided.

Do not attempt more than one set of practice test questions in one day. After completing the first practice test, wait two or three days before attempting the second set of questions.

World History Answer Sheet

1. A B C D 11. A B C D
2. A B C D 12. A B C D
3. A B C D 13. A B C D
4. A B C D 14. A B C D
5. A B C D 15. A B C D
6. A B C D 16. A B C D
7. A B C D 17. A B C D
8. A B C D 18. A B C D
9. A B C D 19. A B C D
10. A B C D 20. A B C D

US History Answer Sheet

1. (A) (B) (C) (D)   11. (A) (B) (C) (D)
2. (A) (B) (C) (D)   12. (A) (B) (C) (D)
3. (A) (B) (C) (D)   13. (A) (B) (C) (D)
4. (A) (B) (C) (D)   14. (A) (B) (C) (D)
5. (A) (B) (C) (D)   15. (A) (B) (C) (D)
6. (A) (B) (C) (D)   16. (A) (B) (C) (D)
7. (A) (B) (C) (D)   17. (A) (B) (C) (D)
8. (A) (B) (C) (D)   18. (A) (B) (C) (D)
9. (A) (B) (C) (D)   19. (A) (B) (C) (D)
10. (A) (B) (C) (D) 20. (A) (B) (C) (D)

Geography Answer Sheet

1. A B C D   11. A B C D
2. A B C D   12. A B C D
3. A B C D   13. A B C D
4. A B C D   14. A B C D
5. A B C D   15. A B C D
6. A B C D   16. A B C D
7. A B C D   17. A B C D
8. A B C D   18. A B C D
9. A B C D   19. A B C D
10. A B C D   20. A B C D

Civics and Government Answer Sheet

1. Ⓐ Ⓑ Ⓒ Ⓓ 11. Ⓐ Ⓑ Ⓒ Ⓓ
2. Ⓐ Ⓑ Ⓒ Ⓓ 12. Ⓐ Ⓑ Ⓒ Ⓓ
3. Ⓐ Ⓑ Ⓒ Ⓓ 13. Ⓐ Ⓑ Ⓒ Ⓓ
4. Ⓐ Ⓑ Ⓒ Ⓓ 14. Ⓐ Ⓑ Ⓒ Ⓓ
5. Ⓐ Ⓑ Ⓒ Ⓓ 15. Ⓐ Ⓑ Ⓒ Ⓓ
6. Ⓐ Ⓑ Ⓒ Ⓓ 16. Ⓐ Ⓑ Ⓒ Ⓓ
7. Ⓐ Ⓑ Ⓒ Ⓓ 17. Ⓐ Ⓑ Ⓒ Ⓓ
8. Ⓐ Ⓑ Ⓒ Ⓓ 18. Ⓐ Ⓑ Ⓒ Ⓓ
9. Ⓐ Ⓑ Ⓒ Ⓓ 19. Ⓐ Ⓑ Ⓒ Ⓓ
10. Ⓐ Ⓑ Ⓒ Ⓓ 20. Ⓐ Ⓑ Ⓒ Ⓓ

Economics Answer Sheet

1. A B C D   11. A B C D
2. A B C D   12. A B C D
3. A B C D   13. A B C D
4. A B C D   14. A B C D
5. A B C D   15. A B C D
6. A B C D   16. A B C D
7. A B C D   17. A B C D
8. A B C D   18. A B C D
9. A B C D   19. A B C D
10. A B C D   20. A B C D

Social Studies Skills and Concepts

1. Ⓐ Ⓑ Ⓒ Ⓓ   11. Ⓐ Ⓑ Ⓒ Ⓓ
2. Ⓐ Ⓑ Ⓒ Ⓓ   12. Ⓐ Ⓑ Ⓒ Ⓓ
3. Ⓐ Ⓑ Ⓒ Ⓓ   13. Ⓐ Ⓑ Ⓒ Ⓓ
4. Ⓐ Ⓑ Ⓒ Ⓓ   14. Ⓐ Ⓑ Ⓒ Ⓓ
5. Ⓐ Ⓑ Ⓒ Ⓓ   15. Ⓐ Ⓑ Ⓒ Ⓓ
6. Ⓐ Ⓑ Ⓒ Ⓓ   16. Ⓐ Ⓑ Ⓒ Ⓓ
7. Ⓐ Ⓑ Ⓒ Ⓓ   17. Ⓐ Ⓑ Ⓒ Ⓓ
8. Ⓐ Ⓑ Ⓒ Ⓓ   18. Ⓐ Ⓑ Ⓒ Ⓓ
9. Ⓐ Ⓑ Ⓒ Ⓓ   19. Ⓐ Ⓑ Ⓒ Ⓓ
10. Ⓐ Ⓑ Ⓒ Ⓓ   20. Ⓐ Ⓑ Ⓒ Ⓓ

Part I - US History

1. Why was the "Gilded Age" called the Gilded Age?

    a. the California Gold Rush happened during it

    b. Gold was the major status symbol at the time

    c. There was a class of super-rich who enjoyed a lavish life-style, while there were many in extreme poverty

    d. Gangsters would gild enemies that were rich and/or greedy

2. What was the "Great Migration" of the United states in the early 1900s and late 1800s?

    a. Many blacks moving out of the South

    b. Large groups of European immigrants moving to the East Coast of the United States through Ellis Island

    c. Asians immigrating to the West Coast of the United States

    d. The last large movement of Native Americans to reservations

3. What created woman's suffrage in the United States?

    a. The Seneca Falls Convention

    b. The 18th Amendment

    c. The 19th Amendment

    d. The Jeannette Rankin Law

4. Who built the Panama Canal?

    a. The French

    b. The United States

    c. The Spanish

    d. Both A and B

5. What was the Open Door Policy?

a. All countries would lower tariffs for more open markets

b. Anyone could propose an idea to the president through the mail

c. China would be open to trade with all countries

d. A name coined for how people would go from government positions to being employed by the companies that lobbied them when they retired

6. What did the Federal Reserve Act do?

a. Gave legal authority to issue U.S. Dollars

b. Set up a government bank

c. All banks had to keep at least 10% of their capital liquid

d. Took United States assets out of private hands and put it in public trusts

7. What contributed to the United States joining World War I?

a. The bombing of Pearl Harbor

b. Alliances with Britain and France

c. German U-boats torpedoing United States ships

d. Both B and C

8. What did the Dawes Plan do?

a. Gave aid in the form of tools and materials to Europe for reconstruction

b. Gave money to Germany to pay war reparations to the Allies

c. Facilitated the immigration of displaced persons at the end of World War I to the United States in exchange for a certain amount of low paid labor

d. Gave money to countries who promised to fight communism

9. What was the start of the Great Depression?

  a. Prohibition

  b. The stock market collapse of 1929

  c. Germany defaulting on its loans to the United States after World War I

  d. The Dust Bowl

10. What did World War II unquestionably do for the US Economy?

  a. End the Great Depression

  b. Reduce unemployment

  c. Exacerbate the Great Depression

  d. Choices A and B are still up to debate

11. What caused the Great Depression?

  a. Excessive borrowing

  b. Restricting the amount of money in the economy

  c. People not spending money

  d. All of the above

12. What caused the global trade to collapse during the Great Depression?

  a. Smoot-Hawley Tariff Act

  b. Revolutions in many developing nations

  c. Black Tuesday

  d. The Nazis and similar fascist groups taking power in many countries

13. Which one of these did President Roosevelt NOT implement to help end the Great Depression?

    a. Federally insure banks

    b. Social Security

    c. Pay people back who lost their bank accounts in the crash

    d. Repeal prohibition

14. Which of these did NOT end during the Great Depression?

    a Adherence to the Gold Standard

    b. Prohibition

    c. The Dust Bowl

    d. Tennessee Valley Authority

15. What were Roosevelt's "Fireside Chats?"

    a. Radio addresses to the nation explaining what he was doing

    b. Thirty talks with different world leaders to try and lessen the effects of the Great Depression

    c. Shows that Roosevelt put on for the newly invented television that endeared him to the nation

    d. Secret talks with key members of industry to try and reinvigorate the economy

16. Why did the United States enter the Pacific War in World War II?

    a. They were asked by France for support

    b. The Japanese bombed Pearl Harbor

    c. Germany declared War on Great Britain, whom the United States was allied to

    d. They felt morally compelled to fight against Germany

17. Which two Japanese cities did the United States bomb during World War II?

    a. Hiroshima and Osaka

    b. Nagasaki and Hokkaido

    c. Hokkaido and Osaka

    d. Hiroshima and Nagasaki

18. Who was the United States president during World War II?

    a. Woodrow Wilson

    b. Herbert Hoover

    c. Harry Truman

    d. Franklin Roosevelt

19. What did Rosie the Riveter encourage women to do during World War II?

    a. To work in factories

    b. To join the military

    c. To support men in the workplace and military

    d. To work producing food

20. What was one reason the Allied forces triumphed over the Axis powers in World War II?

    a. The Allied forces were more organized

    b. The Allied forces produced more supplies

    c. The Allied forces new all the Axis powers plans in advance

    d. The Allied forces were more technologically advanced

Part II - World History

1. What was the motive of the Great Game between Russia and Great Britain during the New Imperialism colonization of Asia?

    a. To secure clear paths to countries like India, Iran and Afghanistan

    b. To financially exhaust each others countries

    c. To establish trade routes across Asia to Japan and Korea

    d. To be the first to secure trade agreements with most of Asia

2. What was one thing achieved with the Glorious Revolution in Great Britain in 1688?

    a. A Catholic monarch was removed from the throne

    b. A new social order demanding economic equality

    c. New industrial machines that lowered the cost of goods

    d. The standardization of education which allowed everyone to go to school

3. What was the main industry of the Industrial Revolution?

    a. Glass

    b. Paper

    c. Textiles

    d. Gas lighting

4. Which was the first European colony to declare its independence?

    a. Haiti

    b. The United States

    c. Chile

    d. Mexico

5. Which event is considered to be the start of the French Revolution?

    a. The rise of Napoleon Bonaparte

    b. The Woman's March on Versailles

    c. The passing of The Declaration of the Rights of Man and of the Citizen

    d. The storming of the Bastille

6. Which famous American directly influenced the writing of The Declaration of the Rights of Man and of the Citizen in France?

    a. John Adams

    b. George Washington

    c. Thomas Jefferson

    d. Benjamin Franklin

7. Which of these was NOT a cause of the Bolshevik Revolution?

    a. Lack of technological advancement in agriculture

    b. Lack of education and health care

    c. Spread of Marxist ideas

    d. Inspiration from the American Revolution

8. Which of these was NOT a consequence of the Bolshevik Revolution?

    a. Women in Russia gained the right to vote

    b. Russia became a super power

    c. The Cold War

    d. The royal family went into hiding

9. Which of these was NOT included in the Government of India Act introduced by Britain in 1935?

a. It set up eleven provincial assemblies that had local control of government

b. It give India a say in its domestic affairs

c. It addressed the political disputes between Hindus and Muslims

d. It introduced direct elections

10. Who is considered to be the founding father of Pakistan?

a. Muhammad Jinnah

b. Jawaharial Nehru

c. Choudhary Rahmat Ali

d. Mahatma Gandhi

11. Which of these was NOT one of Sun Yat-sen's, president of the Republic of China, Three Principles for the governing of China?

a. Nationalism

b. Capitalism

c. Socialism

d. Democracy

12. Which of these is NOT true of the Boxer Rebellion in China in 1900?

a. It failed

b. It was a peaceful rebellion

c. It was to expel European powers from China

d. It was to overthrow the Manchu dynasty

13. What did the Balfour Declaration of 1917 say?

a. Great Britain had control of Palestine following World War I

b. Great Britain would support the creation of a Jewish homeland in Palestine

c. Great Britain would give Palestine to the Arabs at the end of World War I

d. Arabs and Jews would need to share Palestine

14. What was the Treaty of Sevres of 1920?

a. A peace treaty that ended the Ottoman Empire after WWI

b. A treaty by France granting self governance to Syria after WWI

c. A peace treaty between France and Germany at the end of WWI

d. A treaty between France and Britain to remain allies following WWI

15. What type of government was instated in Italy under Benito Mussolini in Italy after World War I?

a. Totalitarianism

b. Socialism

c. Democracy

d. Fascism

16. Who won the Spanish Civil War?

a. No side one, the war was interrupted by WWII

b. The Republican Popular Front

c. The Nationalists led by Francisco Franco

d. King Alphonso XIII

17. Which of these is NOT true of World War I?

a. It led to the creation of new nations

b. It used modern technology such as guns and tanks

c. It was the result of strong Nationalism in European countries

d. It was fought almost entirely on land

18. What was the immediate cause of WWI?

a. An increased militarism in Europe

b. The murder of Archduke Francis Ferdinand of Austria

c. National rivalries between countries following the Balkan Wars

d. A secret system of alliances between European countries

19. How was the Treaty of Versailles a cause of World War II?

a. It angered many Germans who were willing to look to Hitler to end the Treaty

b. It did not put strict enough ties on Germany's military power

c. It created a system of alliances that dragged multiple countries into WWII

d. It was a peace treaty that prevented any nation from attacking Germany

20. Which United States president was influential in the peace talks following World War I?

a. Woodrow Wilson

b. William Taft

c. Warren Harding

d. Franklin Roosevelt

Part III - Geography

1. In which direction has the mainland U.S. expanded since the American Revolution?

    a. northward

    b. southward

    c. eastward

    d. westward

2. Which of the following will humans not normally avoid?

    a. cold weather

    b. warm weather

    c. deserts

    d. high altitudes

3. Immigrants to the U.S. have always

    a. been welcomed with open arms by the native-born population

    b. been enslaved

    c. been discriminated against before finding equality

    d. come from Latin America

4. Diffusion which moves a trend from one leader to another throughout a geographic area is known as

    a. expansion diffusion

    b. stimulus diffusion

    c. relocation diffusion

    d. hierarchical diffusion

5. What country has the U.S. military occupied from 2001 until 2011?

    a. Afghanistan

    b. Iraq

    c. Israel

    d. Lebanon

6. The science of mapmaking is

    a. archaeology

    b. cartography

    c. geography

    d. GPS

7. What is environmental determinism?

    a. countries establishing rules to determine land usage

    b. human devastation of the environment

    c. environments have pre-determined uses which can only be altered by man

    d. climate and landforms are responsible for differences in human culture

8. Limited resources generally lead to

    a. a dense population

    b. exploitation by industrial businesses

    c. a trade route

    d. a scattered population

9. Which region of the U.S. has the fastest growing population?

    a. the northeast

    b. the southeast

    c. the northwest

    d. the Midwest

10. A farmer that produces enough food for his or her family and nothing more is known as a

    a. Subsistence farmer.

    b. Entrepreneur.

    c. Businessman.

    d. Migrant farm worker.

11. What is the main reason that food production societies won out over hunting and gathering societies?

    a. societies that produce food are more intelligent

    b. societies that produce food can support more people

    c. societies that produce food have less disease

    d. societies that produce food are more mobile

12. Agriculture is best defined as

    a. hunting for animals, fishing, or gathering plants

    b. deliberate cultivation of plants and raising of animals for food or economic gain

    c. the use of technology to increase production

    d. altering the genetic material of plants and animals

13. The process by which wild animals were utilized for human benefit is

    a. agriculture.

    b. domestication.

    c. hearth.

    d. agribusiness.

14. Country A has a territory of 5,000 square kilometers with 100 people per square kilometer. Country B has a territory of 10,000 square kilometers with 80 people per square kilometer.

Which country has a higher population?

    a. country A

    b. country B

    c. the populations are equal

    d. there is no way to determine their populations from this information

15. Which of the following countries has the highest population density?

    a. Russia

    b. Canada

    c. India

    d. Turkey

16. Where is Honduras located?

    a. South America

    b. Central America

    c. Asia

    d. Africa

17. What is an epicenter?

    a. The spot where an earthquake originates.

    b. The spot on the earth's surface directly above where an earthquake originates.

    c. The estimated area where an earthquake has taken place.

    d. The center of the earthquake.

18. Name the lines that run east and west around the globe.

    a. Longitude

    b., Equator

    c. Latitude

    jd. Greenwich Mean Line

19. What is the name of the supercontinent that broke apart to create the continents that we know today?

    a. Pangaea

    b. Gondwana

    c. Ur

    d. Laurasia

20. Which country is not a part of the Pacific Rim?

    a. United States

    b. Japan

    c. Australia

    d. England

Part IV - Civics and Government

1. The main purpose of dividing the government into three branches is

    a. so that no one branch could become too powerful.

    b. so that at least one branch could survive in case of an attack.

    c. to triple the strength of the government.

    d. to take away power from the military.

2. What is the minimum age to serve in the House of Representatives?

    a. 35

    b. 30

    c. 25

    d. 18

3. How does a bill become a law?

    a. It passes through the Senate and is then signed by the President

    b. It is signed by the President and is then passed by Parliament

    c. It passes through both houses of Congress and is vetoed by the President

    d. It passes through both houses of Congress and is signed by the President

4. How can congress override a presidential veto?

    a. With a 2/3 majority vote

    b. With a simple majority vote

    c. With a reconciliation bill

    d. There is no way to override a presidential veto

5. How is an amendment added to the Constitution?

    a. With a majority vote in Congress and the President's signature

    b. With 3/4 of the states ratifying it

    c. With a 2/3 majority vote in Congress

    d. With a majority of the popular vote

6. How many days (excluding Sundays) does the President have to sign a bill into law?

    a. 10
    b. 5
    c. 30
    d. 90

7. How many senators represent each state?

    a. 2
    b. 3
    c. it depends on the state's geographical size
    d. it depends on the size of the state's population

8. Whose vote breaks a tie in the Senate?

    a. The President
    b. The Vice President
    c. The Speaker of the House
    d. The Supreme Court

9. How many congressmen represent each state?

    a. 2
    b. 3
    c. It depends on the state's geographical size
    d. It depends on the size of the state's population

10. The U.S. Constitution designed the legislature to be bicameral. What does bicameral mean?

    a. There are two political parties
    b. There are three branches of government
    c. There are two levels of government: state and federal
    d. There are two houses of Congress

11. Freedom of speech and freedom of religion are guaranteed in which constitutional amendment?

    a. The first
    b. The second
    c. The third
    d. The fourth

12. The right to bear arms is guaranteed in the

    a. Declaration of Independence
    b. Bill of Rights
    c. Magna Carta
    d. Articles of Confederation

13. The right to habeas corpus guarantees that you cannot be arrested and held by the police unless

    a. you broke the law.
    b. you are charged with a crime.
    c. you are an American citizen.
    d. you are given a phone call.

14. Citizens can be summoned to court to serve as a member of a

    a. jury.
    b. counsel.
    c. association.
    d. law firm.

15. A demand to appear in court as a witness is called a

    a. verdict.
    b. accusation.
    c. ruling.
    d. subpoena.

16. What does "to plead the Fifth Amendment refers to?"

    a. The right to bear arms

    b. The right to an education

    c. The right not to incriminate yourself in court

    d. The right to have an attorney in court

17. Government officials in the U.S. are

    a. legally protected from prosecution for crimes.

    b. never investigated for crimes or misdeeds.

    c. protected by diplomatic immunity.

    d. subject to the same laws as other citizens.

18. The Bill of Rights prohibits excessive bail, excessive fines and what type of punishment?

    a. Corporal punishment

    b. Capital punishment

    c. Collateral punishment

    d. Cruel and unusual punishment

19. American women were given the right to vote in

    a. 1776

    b. 1820

    c. 1920

    d. 1980

20. The right to vote is also known as

    a. segregation.

    b. taxation.

    c. counsel.

    d. suffrage.

Part V - Economics

1. The Securities and Exchange Commission regulates

    a. Agriculture

    b. Homeland Security

    c. The national budget

    d. The stock market

2. Federal income tax is

    a. Paid every time you buy something

    b. Paid through fees for government services

    c. Due annually, although it is normally deducted from every paycheck

    d. Due when you receive a government service

3. Which of the following is a good example of a public good?

    a. A park

    b. A plumber

    c. An airline

    d. A taxi

4. Sales tax is

    a. Paid every time you buy something

    b. Paid through fees for government services

    c. Due annually, although it is normally deducted from every paycheck

    d. Due when you receive a government service

5. Which of the following are exempt from federal taxes?

a. Large corporations
b. Small businesses
c. Athletes
d. Religious institutions

6. The federal government gets its funding by

a. Taxation
b. Selling goods
c. Investing in stocks
d. Donations

7. During the Great Depression, Keynesian economics was employed to

a. raise taxes and decrease government spending.
b. lower taxes and decrease government spending.
c. raise taxes and increase government spending.
d. lower taxes and increase government spending.

8. Bank deposits are guaranteed by the

a. SEC.
b. FDA.
c. HUD.
d. FDIC.

9. If a country's imports have more value than its exports, it is said to have a

a. trade surplus.
b. trade deficit.
c. balance of trade.
d. globalized economy.

10. What is a tariff?

    a. A tax on imports
    b. A fee for government services
    c. A guaranteed bank deposit
    d. A stock

11. Ideally, supply and demand will settle into

    a. a market.
    b. a mutual fund.
    c. a balance of trade.
    d. equilibrium.

12. If demand for a product falls sharply when prices rise, the demand has

    a. high elasticity.
    b. low elasticity.
    c. high supply.
    d. low supply.

13. The immediate effect of taxes on a business or a consumer is

    a. an increase in economic efficiency.
    b. a decrease in economic efficiency.
    c. an increase in elasticity.
    d. a decrease in elasticity.

14. When the government increases the money supply and lowers interest rates, it is trying to do what?

    a. slow down the economy

    b. downsize

    c. allow the economy to correct itself naturally

    d. stimulate economic growth

15. If the government raises taxes and decreases spending, it is engaged in what type of policy?

    a. contractionary

    b. expansionary

    c. speculative

    d. stimulus

16. When the price of a good rises, the quantity of a good rises. When the price falls, the quantity falls. What best describes this relationship?

    a. Supply

    b. Demand

    c. Deficit

    d. Inflation

17. What is the ability of an economy to produce more goods and services than during a previous period is called?

    a. Economic Downturn

    b. Economic Growth

    c. Economic Strength

    d. Economic Weakness

18. What is someone who acquires goods and services for use?

    a. User

    b. Seller

    c. Business

    d. Consumer

19. GDP stands for:

    a. Gross Domestic Profit

    b. Great Domestic Profit

    c. Gross Domicile Proceedings

    d. Gross Domestic Pension

20. When a company earns more money than it spends, they have made a _____.

    a. Loss

    b. Expenditure

    c. Profit

    d. Deposit

Part VI - Social Studies Methods and Concepts

1. What are human constructs that group similar groups of people in one geographic area?

    a. Regions

    b. Countries

    c. Continents

    d. Islands

2. What is the movement of people from rural to urban areas?

    a. Ruralization

    b. Urbanization

    c. Migration

    d. Immigration

3. What are feelings of pride and devotion to your country?

    a. Fanaticism

    b. Jingoism

    c. Nationalism

    d. Absolutism

4. What is one country's domination of another's political and/or economic life?

    a. Capitalism

    b. Socialism

    c. Imperialism

    d. Occupation

5. What are the sum total of an individual's values and attitudes?

    a. Attitude

    b. Identity

    c. Family

    d. Genetic Makeup

6. The ability to understand others because you're able to share their feelings is called:

    a. Sympathy

    b. Pity

    c. Grievance

    d. Empathy

7. Understanding the similarities and differences among various ethnic groups, socioeconomic classes, religions, and other identifying characteristics is called:

    a. Diversity

    b. Range

    c. Empathy

    d. Sympathy

8. Patterns of human behavior (ideas, beliefs, values, etc.) that are transmitted to succeeding generations are called:

    a. Succession

    b. Culture

    c. Evolution

    d. Survival Mechanisms

9. What is the right to select from many alternatives?

    a. Choice

    b. Justice

    c. Alternatives

    d. Live

10. A clash of ideas from incompatible forces is called:

    a. Conflict

    b. Choice

    c. War

    d. Justice

11. Trying to evoke an alteration in ideas or events is trying to elicit _____.

    a. Conflict

    b. Choice

    c. Change

    d. Justice

12. What is the the movement of people to a new country?

    a. Immigration

    b. Migration

    c. Urbanization

    d. Ruralizing

13. What is the movement of people from one place to another, with the purpose of settling either temporarily or permanently called?

    a. Immigration

    b. Migration

    c. Urbanization

    d. Ruralizing

14. What is the process when a minority group slowly adapts to the customs and attitudes of the place or culture that they are in called?

    a. Acculturation

    b. Assimilation

    c. Repatriation

    d. Expatriation

15. **What is gaining partial or full control over another country, governing it, while exploiting the country's resources called?**

    a. Imperialism

    b. Dictatorship

    c. Colonialism

    d. Revolution

Answer Key

Part I - US History

1. C
The Gilded Age was a satire given by Mark Twain about how the super-rich were a thin gold varnish covering up societies' woes.

Choice A is incorrect; the California Gold Rush happened before the Gilded Age.

Choice B is incorrect; while having gold was a status symbol it was not the reason why the time period was called the Gilded Age.

Choice D is incorrect; gangsters were never known for gilding their enemies.

2. A
A black exodus from the South to the Midwest intensified during the end of reconstruction and the start of Jim Crow laws.

Choice B is incorrect; while European immigrants were immigrating in large numbers during this time period this was not a name given to it.

Choice C is incorrect; Asian immigrants were immigrating during this time period and suffered a lot of discrimination through a general hostility to their culture and through official means by way of the Chinese Exclusion Act and the Gentleman's agreement.

Choice D is incorrect; the creation of reservations ended in the mid-1800s under President Hays, new reservation land would not be added until 1934 under the Indian Reorganization Act.

3. C
With the 19th Amendment Women's Suffrage came into na-

tional law in 1919.

Choice A is incorrect; the Seneca Falls Convention was the first women's rights conventions, it did not actually create any laws though.

Choice B is incorrect; the 18th Amendment to the United States Constitution prohibited the manufacture, sale, transport, import, or export of alcoholic beverages.

Choice D is incorrect; Jeannette Rankin was the first women senator in the United States, before all women had the right to vote, but she never had a law named after her.

4. D
Both the French and the United States contributed to building the Panama Canal, though there was about a decade where there was no construction.

Choice A is incorrect; while the French did start construction of the Panama Canal in 1881, they did not complete it.

Choice B is incorrect; the United States finished the Panama Canal in 1914, but they did not start the construction.

Choice C is incorrect; the Spanish did not contribute to building the Panama Canal.

5. C
Secretary of State John Hay proposed the Open Door Policy to his European counterparts to abate any conflict between powers over China in the future.

Choice A is incorrect; no countries willingly lowered tariffs significantly during the early 20th century when the Open Door Policy took effect.

Choice B is incorrect; President Mckinley did not accept ideas from everyone when the Open Door Policy took effect.

Choice D is incorrect; the revolving door is the name coined for people going from government positions to industry positions they were supposed to regulate and vice versa.

6. A
Before the Federal Reserve Act, banks did not have the authority to put money into, or take money out of circulation. Choice B is incorrect; there has not been a government bank in the United States since 1836, the Second Bank of the United States.

Choice C is incorrect; laws have been fluid over the years on how much cash a bank must have liquid, and will probably continue to be so.

Choice D is incorrect; The United States has taken assets out of private hands and put them in public trusts, but the Federal Reserve Act did not do this.

7. C
The Germans had a submarine blockade of Great Britain and torpedoed many ships, both merchant and passenger liners, angering many Americans and was a major factor in America entering the war.

Choice A is incorrect; the bombing of Pearl harbor is what led the United States into World War II.

Choice B is incorrect; the United States was not allied with either Britain or France.

8. B
To allow the Allies to pay off their debts to the United States, the United States loaned money to Germany so that they could pay off their reparations to the Allies.

Choice A is incorrect; this is the Marshall Plan after World War II.

Choice C is incorrect; the United Sates actually slowed down immigration to the United States instead of increasing it.

Choice D is incorrect; this is the Truman Doctrine after World War II.

9. B
The United States stock market collapse of 1929 caused the

downfall of many financial institutions and the start of the Great Depression.

Choice A is incorrect; Prohibition started in the 1920s, the Great Depression did not start until 1929.

Choice C is incorrect; while Germany did default on its loans to the United States after World War I, the Great Depression occurred several years after this event.

Choice D is incorrect; the Dust Bowl happened during the Great Depression, it did not precipitate it.

10. B
World War II reduced unemployment with so many working-class men in the armed forces, and jobs were available for anyone able to take them.

Choice A is incorrect; the Great Depression ended with the start of World War II, but the economy was already recovering, so there is some doubt as to whether it helped end the depression.

Choice C is incorrect; World War II did not exacerbate the Great Depression because the Great Depression ended with the onset of World War II.

Choice D is incorrect; only the ending of the Great Depression is up for debate.

11. D
A culmination of the answers given and a few others were what caused the Great Depression.

Choice A is incorrect; excessive borrowing was partly to blame for causing the Great Depression, but it would not have been as severe if other things had not also happened.

Choice B is incorrect; restricting the amount of money ensured that people would not be able to pay off their debts as easily, but even that by itself would not have caused the Great Depression.

Choice C is incorrect; with people not spending money the economy continued to slump, but that would not have been severe enough to cause the Great Depression.

12. A
The Smoot-Hawley Tariff Act and the many retaliatory tariffs around the world closed down international trade.

Choice B is incorrect; while there were some revolutions in developing nations, they did not have a significant impact on world trade.

Choice C is incorrect; Black Tuesday was the start of the Great Depression.

Choice D is incorrect; fascist groups taking power did not have an effect on world trade.

13. C
Most people who had money in a bank lost it with no compensation during the Great Depression.

Choice A is incorrect; President Roosevelt set up a program to insure banks that is still in existence today.

Choice B is incorrect; President Roosevelt set up a Social Security administration that is still in effect today.

Choice D is incorrect; President Roosevelt repealed prohibition to increase revenue and decrease the amount spent on enforcement.

14. D
The Tennessee Valley Authority still exists as a government utility company, but is not connected with the ending of the Great Depression.

Choice A is incorrect; the Gold Standard was ended during the Great Depression by all first world nations because so many people were demanding gold in exchange for money that governments would go bankrupt otherwise.

Choice B is incorrect; Prohibition was formally ended during the Great Depression due to its unpopularity and the increased revenue and decreased expenditures from enforcement.

Choice C is incorrect; the Dust Bowl ended in 1940 right before the end of the Great Depression.

15. A
Roosevelt started "Fireside Chats" to let the nation know what was happening and relieve their fears.

Choice B is incorrect; while Roosevelt did work with world leaders, but these were not called fireside chats.

Choice C is incorrect; the television was not yet invented.

Choice D is incorrect; while Roosevelt did have many talks with members of industry, these were not his fireside chats.

16. B
The US entered the Pacific War, declaring war on Japan after Japan bombed Pearl Harbor.

Choice A is incorrect; the United States did not enter WWII to support France.

Choice C is incorrect; the United States was not allied with Great Britain.

Choice D is incorrect; that is not why the United States entered WWII.

17. D
The United States dropped atomic bombs on Hiroshima and Nagasaki.

Choice A is incorrect; the United States bombed Hiroshima, but not Osaka.

Choice B is incorrect; the United States bombed Nagasaki, but not Hokkaido.

Choice C is incorrect; the United States did not bomb Osaka or Hokkaido.

18. D
Franklin Roosevelt was president for most of WWII.

Choice A is incorrect; Woodrow Wilson was president during WWI.

Choice B is incorrect; Herbert Hoover was president before WWII.

Choice C is incorrect; Harry Truman was president for the end of WWII.

19. A
The propaganda campaign, Rosie the Riveter, was to encourage women to work in factories producing wartime supplies.

Choice B is incorrect; women did join the military, but Rosie the Riveter did not encourage this.

Choice C is incorrect; Rosie the Riveter did not encourage to support men in the war effort.

Choice D is incorrect; Rosie the Riveter did not encourage woman to product food.

20. B
The allied forces were successful because the United States was able to produce and provide most of the wartime supplies needed to win the war.

Choice A is incorrect; the Allied forces were not more organized.

Choice C is incorrect; the Allied forces did not know all their enemies plans.

Choice D is incorrect; the Allies were not more technologically advanced than the Axis powers.

Part II - World History

1. A
By controlling Central and Southern Asia, other countries would be easily accessible.

Choice B is incorrect; neither country was trying to financially exhaust the other.

Choice C is incorrect; neither country was trying to trade with Japan.

Choice D is incorrect; Britain and Russia were not competing for trade in Asia.

2. A
The Catholic King James II of England was overthrown by the Protestant William of Orange.

Choice B is incorrect; the Glorious Revolution did not achieve economic equality.

Choice C is incorrect; implementation of industrial machines was during the Industrial Revolution.

Choice D is incorrect; the Glorious Revolution did not impact education.

3. C
Increased productivity due to the cotton gin, power looms, the flying shuttle and the spinning jenny made textile production the leading industry of the Industrial Revolution

Choice A is incorrect; glass was produced, but it was not the main industry.

Choice B is incorrect; paper was produced, but it was not the main industry.

Choice D is incorrect; gas lighting was produced, but it was not the main industry.

4. B
The United States was the first European colony to declare its independence from Britain in 1776.

Choice A is incorrect; Haiti declared its independence from France in 1804.

Choice C is incorrect; Chile was independent of Spain by 1831.

Choice D is incorrect; Mexico was independent of Spain by 1831.

5. D
The storming of the Bastille happened in July, 1789 and is considered the flash point of the French Revolution.

Choice A is incorrect; Napoleon's rise to power is considered to be the end of the French Revolution.

Choice B is incorrect; the March on Versailles happened during the French Revolution when people were upset with the high price of bread.

Choice C is incorrect; this document was passed in France in August, 1789.

6. C
Thomas Jefferson directly influenced the writing of the Declaration by working with the man who introduced it, General Lafayette.

Choice A is incorrect; John Adams did not directly influence the writing of the Declaration.

Choice B is incorrect; George Washington did not directly influence the writing of the Declaration.

Choice D is incorrect; Benjamin Franklin did not directly influence the writing of the Declaration.

7. D
The American Revolution in 1776 happened much earlier than the Bolshevik Revolution in 1917.

Choice A is incorrect; peasants were upset at having to farm with primitive tools.

Choice B is incorrect; peasants were upset at the lack of social welfare provided by the government.

Choice C is incorrect; the spread of Marxist ideas encouraged people to create new political parties.

8. D
The royal family was placed under house arrest and then killed - they did not go into hiding.

All the other choices were choices were consequences of the revolution, women were given the right to vote, Russia became a world power under Stalin and Lenin and communist ideas spread during the Bolshevik Revolution led to the Cold War with capitalism.

9. C
The Government of India Act introduced by Britain in 1935 did not address how to resolve disputes between Hindus and Muslims.

Choice A is incorrect; the Act did set up provincial governments.

Choice B is incorrect; the Act set up an assembly that gave India a say in most of the country's decisions, but not defense or foreign affairs.

Choice D is incorrect; the Act did set up direct elections.

10. A
Muhammed Jinnah was a Muslim who insisted that a separate state be created for Muslims.

Choice B is incorrect; Jawaharial Nehru was a famous Indian political leader.

Choice C is incorrect; Choudhary Rahmat Ali was a Muslim who helped create Pakistan, but is not considered to be the founding father.

Choice D is incorrect; Mahatma Gandhi was a Indian leader famous for his peaceful protests against the British.

11. B
Yat-sen did not try to promote capitalism in China.

Choice A is incorrect; Sun believed giving China national pride would help free it from foreign rule.

Choice C is incorrect; Sun believed the needs of all people should be met by the people.

Choice D is incorrect; Sun believed China should be democratic.

12. B
The Boxer Rebellion was very violent and many Europeans and Chinese were killed.

Choice A is incorrect; the Boxer Rebellion was eventually crushed by European powers and the Manchus were reinstated in government.

Choice C is incorrect; many Chinese were upset at the amount of control Europe had in China.

Choice D is incorrect; the Manchu government were puppets to the European powers.

13. B
The British Foreign Secretary, Arthur Balfour, promised Palestine to the Jews, in the Balfour Declaration of 1917.

Choice A is incorrect; the League of Nations gave control of Palestine to Britain following World War I.

Choice C is incorrect; Britain promised Palestine to the Arabs in the McMahon Agreement.

Choice D is incorrect; that Arabs and Jews would need to share Palestine was not part of the Declaration.

14. A
The Treaty of Sevres was treaty between the Allies and the Ottoman Empire at the end of WWI that liquidated the Ottoman Empire.

Choice B is incorrect; the Treaty of Sevres was not between France and Syria.

Choice C is incorrect; the Treaty of Sevres was not between France and Germany.

Choice D is incorrect; the Treaty of Sevres was not between France and Britain.

15. D
The dictator Mussolini established a Fascist government in Italy.

Choice A is incorrect; Mussolini did not establish a Totalitarian government in Italy because the Church was still considered to be higher than the government.

Choice B is incorrect; Mussolini did not establish a Socialist government in Italy.

Choice C is incorrect; Mussolini did not establish a Democracy government in Italy.

16. C
The Nationalists won the Spanish Civil War and Franco became a dictator in Spain.

Choice A is incorrect; the Spanish Civil War ended before WWII began.

Choice B is incorrect; the Popular Front lost the Spanish Civil War.

Choice D is incorrect; King Alphonso XIII had previously been exiled to France.

17. D
WWI was fought both on land and at sea.

Choice A is incorrect; new nations were created after WWI such as Austria and Hungary.

Choice B is incorrect; it was one of the first large scale wars to use modern technology which led to larger loss of life and property.

Choice C is incorrect; strong Nationalism in European countries led to hatred of other countries.

18. B
The murder of Archduke Francis Ferdinand of Austria was the spark that set off WWI.

Choice A, C and D are incorrect, these were all causes of WWI, but not the immediate cause.

19. A
The Treaty of Versailles created poverty in Germany, which Hitler sought to change.

Choice B is incorrect; the Treaty of Versailles demilitarized Germany.

Choice C is incorrect; the Treaty of Versailles did not create a system of alliances.

Choice D is incorrect; the Treaty of Versailles did not prevent attacks on Germany.

20. A
Woodrow Wilson was president of the United States during WWI and helped establish the League of Nations after WWI.

Choice B is incorrect; William Taft was the president before Wilson.

Choice C is incorrect; Warren Harding was the president after Wilson.

Choice D is incorrect; Franklin Roosevelt was the president during WWII.

Part III - Geography

1. D
The U.S. has expanded westward all the way to the Pacific Ocean since the American Revolution.

Choice A is incorrect; Canada is to the north.

Choice B is incorrect; the Caribbean and Mexico were and are to the south.

Choice C is incorrect; the Atlantic Ocean was and is to the east.

2. B
Humans do not normally avoid warm weather.

Choice A is incorrect; humans try to avoid cold weather.

Choice C is incorrect; deserts cannot support very much life.

Choice D is incorrect; high altitudes cannot support much life.

3. C
Immigrants to the U.S. have always always been discriminated against before finding equality.

Choice A is incorrect; the native-born population tends not to welcome immigrants.

Choice B is clearly incorrect; slavery has been illegal since 1863.

Choice D is incorrect; immigrants have come from all over the world.

4. D
Diffusion, which moves a trend from one leader to another throughout a geographic area is known as hierarchical diffusion.

Choice A is incorrect; expansion diffusion is the diffusion of people.

Choice B is incorrect but plausible; stimulus diffusion pertains to ideas, but not necessarily to leaders.

Choice C is incorrect; relocation diffusion skips over certain areas.

5. A
The U.S. military occupied Afghanistan since 2001 until June 2011.

Choice B is incorrect; Iraq was invaded in 2003 and U.S. forces have officially left.

Choice C is incorrect; the U.S. has never occupied Israel.

Choice D is incorrect; the US. sent troops to Lebanon in the 1980s, but did not occupy Lebanon.

6. B
The science of mapmaking is called cartography.

Choice A is incorrect; archaeology is the study of human activity in the past.

Choice C is incorrect; geography is a field of science dedicated to the study of the lands, the features, the inhabitants, and the phenomena of the Earth.

Choice D is incorrect; GPS stands for Global Positioning System.

7. D
Environmental determinism is the theory that climate and landforms are responsible for differences in human culture.

Choice A is incorrect; but plausible due to the word "determine."

Choice B is incorrect; human devastation of the environment is an environmental influence on humans.

Choice C is incorrect; this may be true but it is irrelevant to the question.

8. D
Limited resources generally lead to a scattered population, since the area cannot support many people.

Choice A is incorrect; a dense population needs more resources.

Choice B is incorrect; industrial businesses look for an abundance of resources.

Choice C is incorrect; a trade route may appear but this is irrelevant to the question.

9. B
The southeast region of the U.S. has the fastest growing population.

10. A
Subsistence agriculture is self-sufficiency farming in which the farmers focus on growing enough food to feed themselves and their families. The typical subsistence farm has a range of crops and animals needed by the family to feed and clothe themselves during the year.

Choice B is incorrect; entrepreneurs start businesses.

Choice C is incorrect; businesspeople sell things.

Choice D is incorrect; migrant farm workers are employees of other farmers.

11. B
Food production societies won out over hunting and gathering societies because it supports more people.

Choice A is incorrect; food production has no correlation with intelligence.

Choice C is incorrect; societies that produce food actually have had more disease.

Choice D is incorrect; societies that produce food are actually less mobile.

12. B
Agriculture is the science or practice of farming, including cultivation of the soil for the growing of crops and the rearing of animals to provide food, wool, and other products.

Choice A is incorrect; this is the definition of hunting and gathering.

Choice C is incorrect; technology is used, but B is a much better answer.

Choice D is incorrect; plants and animals do get altered in agriculture, but choice B is a much better answer.

13. B
The process by which wild animals were utilized for human benefit is domestication.

Choice A is incorrect; agriculture is too general a term.

Choice D is incorrect; agribusiness began after domestication took place.

14. B
Country A has a territory of 5,000 square kilometers with 100 people per square kilometer.

Country B has a territory of 10,000 square kilometers with 80 people per square kilometer.
Country B would have a population of 800,000 people.

Choice A is incorrect; country A would have population of 500,000 people.

15. C
India has the highest population density.

16. B
Honduras is located in Central America.

17. B
The spot on the surface directly above where the earthquake originates is the epicenter.

Choice A is incorrect. The spot where an earthquake actually originates is deep underground, and the epicenter is above this point.

Choice C is incorrect. The epicenter pinpoints the exact spot on the earth's surface directly above the earthquake, not the general area.

Choice D is incorrect. The epicenter pinpoints the exact spot on the earth's surface directly above the earthquake, not the earthquake's center.

18. C
Latitude lines run east and west around the globe.

Choice A is incorrect. Longitude lines run north and south around the globe.

Choice B is incorrect. The equator is the imaginary line on Earth's surface that divides the Earth into the Northern and Southern Hemispheres.

Choice D is incorrect. The Prime Meridian is 0 degrees longitude.

19. A
Pangaea is the supercontinent that broke apart to create the continents that we know today.

Choice B is incorrect. Gondwana was the name of one of the southern supercontinents that broke off of Pangaea.

Choice C is incorrect. The supercontinent, Ur, predates Pangaea.

Choice D is incorrect. Laurasia was one of the southern supercontinents that broke off of Pangaea.

20. D
England is on the eastern side of the Atlantic Ocean, not a part of the Pacific Rim.

Choice A is incorrect. The western coast of the United States and Hawaii are part of the Pacific Rim.

Choice B is incorrect. Japan is a part of the Pacific Rim.

Choice C is incorrect. Australia is a part of the Pacific Rim.

Part IV - Civics and Government

1. A
The main purpose of dividing government is to prevent one branch from becoming too powerful, and a dictatorship taking hold.

Choice B is incorrect; but may sound plausible to someone unfamiliar with divided government.

Choice C is incorrect; dividing the government does not strengthen it.

Choice D is incorrect; the military has little to do with this.

2. C
The minimum age to serve in the House of Representatives is 25.

Choice A is incorrect; 35 is the minimum age for president.

Choice B is incorrect; 30 is the minimum age for Senators.

Choice D is incorrect; 18 is the age of majority.

3. D
A bill becomes law when it passes through both houses of Congress and is signed by the President.

Choice A is incorrect; a bill must pass through the House and the Senate, and then it can be signed by the President.

Choice B is clearly incorrect because Parliament is part of the English government.

Choice C is incorrect; a veto negates the passage of a law.

4. A
Congress can override a presidential veto with a two-thirds majority vote.

Choice B is incorrect; a simple majority vote is required to pass a bill.

Choice C is incorrect; reconciliation is a legislative process of the United States Senate intended to allow consideration of a budget bill with debate limited to twenty hours under Senate rules. Reconciliation also exists in the United States House of Representatives, but because the House regularly passes rules that constrain debate and amendment, the process has had a less significant impact on that body.

Choice D is incorrect; a veto can be overridden.

5. B
An amendment added to the constitution with three-quarters of the states ratifying it.

Choice A is incorrect; this is the process for a regular bill.

Choice C is incorrect; this is the process to override a veto.

Choice D is incorrect; virtually nothing is decided by national popular vote.

6. A
The president has 10 days (excluding Sundays) to sign a bill into law.

7. A
Each state is represented by two senators.

Choice C is incorrect; but may seem plausible due to house representation being proportional.

Choice D is incorrect; the size of the state's population determines house representation.

8. B
The Vice President is considered president of the Senate, and their vote breaks a tie.

Choice A is incorrect; the President stays separate from congress.

Choice C is incorrect; the Speaker of the House stays separate from the Senate.

Choice D is clearly incorrect because the Supreme Court does not legislate.

9. D
The number of congressmen that represent each state depends on the state's population.

Choice A is incorrect; each state has 2 senators.

Choice C is incorrect but may seem plausible due to representation being proportional to population.

10. D
The U.S. Constitution specifies a bicameral legislature, which means having two branches or chambers.

Choice A is incorrect but may seem plausible due to the prefix bi-.

Choice B is clearly incorrect because bi- means two.

Choice C is incorrect by definition and because there are many levels of government: city, county, state, federal.

11. A
Freedom of speech and freedom of religion are guaranteed in the first amendment.

Choice B is incorrect; the second amendment is the right to bear arms.

Choice C is incorrect; the third amendment has to do with the quartering of soldiers.

Choice D is incorrect; the fourth amendment has to do with personal security.

12. B
The right to bear arms is guaranteed in the Bill of Rights, which contains the 2nd amendment.

Choice A is incorrect; the Declaration of Independence lists grievances against England.

Choice C is incorrect; the Magna Charta did not guarantee any rights for the people.

Choice D is incorrect; the Articles of Confederation predate the Bill of Rights.

13. B
The right to habeas corpus guarantees that if you are held for more than a day, you must be charged with a crime.

Choice A is incorrect; the police can still arrest you.

Choice C is incorrect; non-citizens can be arrested.

Choice D is incorrect; although it may seem plausible since you are given a phone call after an arrest.

14. A
One civic duty of citizenship is that citizens can be summoned to serve on a jury.

Choice B is incorrect; counsel refers to lawyers.

Choice D is clearly incorrect since one must be a lawyer to join a law firm.

15. D
A demand to appear in court as a witness is called a subpoena.

Choice A is incorrect; a verdict is a decision made by a jury.

Choice B is incorrect; witnesses are not the accused.

Choice C is incorrect; a ruling is a decision by a judge.

16. C
The 5th Amendment is the right not to incriminate yourself in court.

Choice A is incorrect; the right to bear arms is in the 2nd amendment.

Choice B is incorrect; the right to an education is not listed in the Bill of Rights.

Choice D is incorrect; although defendants do have the right to have an attorney in court.

17. D
Government officials in the U.S. are lawmakers, but are not above the law.

Choice A is incorrect; officials can be prosecuted.

Choice B is clearly incorrect as lawmakers are often investigated.

Choice C is incorrect; diplomatic immunity applies to foreign diplomats.

18. D
The Bill of Rights prohibits excessive bail, excessive fines and cruel and unusual punishment.

Choice A is incorrect; the Bill of Rights does not mention corporal punishment.

Choice B is incorrect; capital punishment is legal in the U.S.

Choice C is incorrect; "collateral punishment" is not a term related to the Bill of Rights.

19. C
American women were given the right to vote in 1920. It was the 19th amendment.

Choice A is incorrect; 1776 was the year of the Declaration of Independence.

20. D
The right to vote is also known as suffrage.

Choice A is incorrect but not completely unrelated.

Choice B is clearly incorrect.

Choice C is incorrect; counsel refers to lawyers.

Part V - Economics

1. D
The Securities and Exchange Commission, SEC, regulates The stock market.

Choice A is incorrect; the FDA regulates agriculture.

Choice B is incorrect; the Department of Homeland Security is charged protecting the United States from terrorist attacks.

Choice C is incorrect; congress determines the national budget.

2. C
Federal income tax is due annually, although it is normally deducted from every paycheck.

Choice A is incorrect; sales tax is paid every time you buy something.

Choice B is incorrect; fees are distinct from taxes.

Choice D is incorrect; income tax is distinct from government services.

3. A
A park is a good example of a public good. A public good is

a commodity or service that is provided without profit to all members of a society, either by the government or a private individual or organization.

Choices B, C and D are incorrect; a plumber, an airline and a taxi are examples of private services.

4. A
Sales tax is paid every time you buy something.

Choice B is incorrect; fees are distinct from taxes.

Choice C is incorrect; sales tax is paid when you buy something, not annually.

Choice D is incorrect; sales tax is distinct from government services.

5. D
Religious institutions are not subject to federal taxes.

Choices A and B are incorrect; large corporations and small businesses are subject to taxes.

Choice C is incorrect; Athletes are private citizens and are subject to taxes.

6. A
The federal government gets its funding by taxation.
Choice B is incorrect; the government does not sell goods.

Choice C is incorrect; the government rarely invests in stocks.

Choice D is incorrect; the government rarely receives donations.

7. C
During the Great Depression, Keynesian economics prescribed lower taxes and increasing government spending

to stimulated the economy.

Choice A is incorrect; this is the opposite of the Keynesian approach.

Choice B is incorrect; government spending was increased during the Great Depression.

Choice C is incorrect; taxes were not raised during the Great Depression.

8. D
Bank deposits are guaranteed by the Federal Deposit Insurance Corporation.

Choice A is incorrect; the SEC regulates the stock market.

Choice B is incorrect; the FDA regulates food and drugs.

Choice C is incorrect; HUD is the department of Housing and Urban Development.

9. B
If a country's imports have more value than its exports, it is said to have a trade deficit.

Choice A is incorrect; a trade surplus is the opposite.

Choice C is incorrect; the balance of trade is the difference between imports and exports.

Choice D is incorrect; globalization simply refers to the connectedness of the world's economies.

10. A
A tariff is a tax on imports.

Choice B is incorrect; a tariff is a tax on imports.

Choice C is incorrect; tariffs have little to do with bank deposits.

Choice D is incorrect; tariffs are not related to stocks.

11. D
Ideally, supply and demand will settle into equilibrium.

Choice A may seem plausible, but market is too general and choice D is a better answer.

Choice B is is irrelevant, but plausible because of the word "mutual."

Choice C is incorrect; balance of trade refers to imports and exports.

12. A
If demand for a product falls sharply when prices rise, the demand has high elasticity. Elasticity is the influence of prices on demand.

Choice B is incorrect; if the demand had low elasticity price would not fall sharply.

Choice C is incorrect; supply is not related.

Choice D is incorrect; supply has little to do with this situation.

13. B
The immediate effect of taxes on a business or a consumer is a decrease in economic efficiency.

Choice A is incorrect; the opposite is true.

Choices C and D are incorrect; elasticity isn't relevant.

14. D
When the government increases the money supply and lowers interest rates, this policy is designed to stimulate economic growth.

Choice A is incorrect; the opposite is true.

Choice B is incorrect; downsizing is unrelated to this situation.

Choice C is incorrect; to allow the economy to correct itself naturally the government would do nothing.

15. A
If the government raises taxes and decreases spending, it is engaged in a contractionary policy.

Choice B is incorrect; expansionary policy lowers taxes and increases spending.

Choice C is incorrect; speculation sounds plausible but has little to do with this situation.

Choice D is incorrect; stimulus would involve expansionary policy.

16. A
Supply is one of the fundamental laws of economics.

Choice B is incorrect. The law of demand states that when the price of a good rises, its demand falls. When the price falls, the demand rises.

Choice C is incorrect. Having more expenses than income is a deficit.

Choice D is incorrect. Inflation is the rise in prices relative to the amount of money in circulation.

17. B
The ability of an economy to produce more goods than a previous period is called an economic growth.

Choice A is incorrect. An economic downturn is when the economy starts to slow down.

Choice C is incorrect. Though economic strength is related to the amount of goods it can produce, does not measure between periods.

Choice D is incorrect. The inability to produce many goods and having a weak economy is considered an economic weakness.

18. D
Consumers acquire goods and services for their use.

Choice A is incorrect. A user uses goods and services, but it is not the correct answer.

Choice B is incorrect. A seller sells goods and services.

Choice C is incorrect. Businesses provide and/or sell goods and services.

19. A
GDP stands for Gross Domestic Profit.

Choice B in incorrect. Great Domestic Profit is not a term that exists.

Choice C is incorrect. Gross Domicile Proceedings is not a term that exists.

Choice D is incorrect. Gross Domestic Pension is not a term that exists.

20. C
When a company earns more than it spends, they make a profit.

Choice A is incorrect. A company makes a loss when they spend more than they earn.

Choice B is incorrect. An expenditure is when a company pays for an expense.

Choice D is incorrect. A deposit is an amount of money put in a bank account.

Part VI - Social Studies Concepts and Methods

1. A
Regions are human constructs that group similar groups of people in one geographic area.

Choice B is incorrect; Countries are artificial borders that group people together. A country is a type of region.

Choice C is incorrect; Continents are very large landmasses.

Choice D is incorrect; Islands are surrounded by water on four sides.

2. B
Urbanization is the movement of people from rural to urban areas.

Choice A is incorrect; Ruralization is the movement of people from urban to rural areas.

Choice C is incorrect; Migration is the temporary or permanent movement by people from one place or another to settle.

Choice D is incorrect; Immigration is the movement of people into a country that they are not native to.

3. C
Feeling pride and devotion to your country is called nationalism.

Choice A is incorrect; Fanaticism involves obsessive enthusiasm for something.

Choice B is incorrect; Jingoism is aggressive foreign policy as a form of extreme patriotism.

Choice D is incorrect; Absolutism is the belief in absolute political, philosophical, and ethical principles.

4. C
One country's domination of another country's political and/or economic life is called imperialism.

Choice A is incorrect; Capitalism is an economic and political system where trade and industry are controlled by private owners.

Choice B is incorrect; Socialism is a social and economic system where the means of production is socially owned.

Choice D is incorrect; Occupation is the activity of living and using a particular place.

5. B
Identity is your own values and attitudes.

Choice A is incorrect; Attitude is the way a person thinks or feels about something.

Choice C is incorrect; Your values do not create your family.

Choice D is incorrect; Your values are not ingrained in your genetic makeup.

6. D
Empathy is your ability to understand others because you're able to share their feelings.

Choice A is incorrect; Sympathy is the act of feeling sorry for someone or something.

Choice B is incorrect; Pity is a strong feeling of sadness for someone or something.

Choice C is incorrect; A grievance is a general feeling of having been treated unfairly.

7. A
Diversity is known as understanding the similarities and differences among various ethnic groups, socioeconomic classes, religions, and other identifying characteristics.

Choice B is incorrect; A range is a group of different things that are similar in some ways.

8. B
Culture is patterns of human behavior (ideas, beliefs, values, etc.) that are transmitted to succeeding generations.

Choice A is incorrect; Succession is a series of things that come one after another.

Choice C is incorrect; Evolution is slow change and/or development.

Choice D is incorrect; Survival mechanisms are behavioral patterns that are selected and reinforced across generations.

9. A
Choice is your right to select from different alternatives.

Choice B is incorrect; Justice happens when individuals are given fair treatment in personal, societal, and governmental interactions.

10. A
Conflict is a clash of ideas from incompatible forces.

Choice B is incorrect; Choice is your right to select from different alternatives.

Choice C is incorrect; War is a prolonged conflict between two parties, usually countries or groups of people.

Choice D is incorrect; Justice happens when individuals are given fair treatment in personal, societal, and governmental interactions.

11. C
Change is trying to evoke an alteration in ideas or events.

Choice A is incorrect; Conflict is a clash of ideas from incompatible forces.

Choice B is incorrect; Choice is your right to select from

many alternatives.

Choice D is incorrect; Justice happens when individuals are given fair treatment in personal, societal, and governmental interactions.

12. A
Immigration is the movement of people into a country that they are not native to.

Choice B is incorrect; Migration is the temporary or permanent movement by people from one place or another to settle.

Choice C is incorrect; Urbanization is the movement of people from rural to urban areas.

Choice D is incorrect; Ruralizing is the movement of people from urban to rural areas.

13. B
Migration is the temporary or permanent movement by people from one place or another to settle.

Choice A is incorrect; Immigration is the movement of people into a country that they are not native to.

Choice C is incorrect; Urbanization is the movement of people from rural to urban areas.

Choice D is incorrect; Ruralizing is the movement of people from urban to rural areas.

14. B
Assimilation is defined as when a minority group slowly adapts to the customs and attitudes of the place or culture that they are in.

Choice A is incorrect; Acculturation is the process of cultural change that happens when cultures meet.

Choice C is incorrect; Repatriation is the process of returning a person to the place of citizenship.

Choice D is incorrect; Expatriation is the process of withdrawing from your native country.

15. C
Gaining partial or full control over another country and governing it, while exploiting the country's resources is called colonialism.

Choice A is incorrect; Imperialism is the policy of giving a country power through diplomacy or military force.
Choice B is incorrect; A dictatorship is a country ruled by a dictator.

Choice D is incorrect; Revolution is a change in power that takes place over a short period of time, often by force.

Conclusion

ONGRATULATIONS! You have made it this far because you have applied yourself diligently to practicing for the exam and no doubt improved your potential score considerably! Getting into a good school is a huge step in a journey that might be challenging at times but will be many times more rewarding and fulfilling. That is why being prepared is so important.

Good Luck!

FREE Ebook Version

Download a FREE Ebook version of the publication!

Suitable for tablets, iPad, iPhone, or any smart phone.

Go to http://tinyurl.com/qykeq2l

Learn to increase your score using time-tested secrets for answering multiple choice questions!

This practice book has everything you need to know about answering multiple choice questions on a standardized test!

You will learn 12 strategies for answering multiple choice questions and then practice each strategy with over 45 reading comprehension multiple choice questions, with extensive commentary from exam experts!

Maybe you have read this kind of thing before, and maybe feel you don't need it, and you are not sure if you are going to buy this book.

Remember though, it only a few percentage points divide the PASS from the FAIL students.

Even if our multiple choice strategies increase your score by a few percentage points, isn't that worth it?

Paperback

www.ingramcontent.com/pod-product-compliance
Lightning Source LLC
LaVergne TN
LVHW051605070426
835507LV00021B/2771